Old Alec, our friend and ne... talk to us as he cycled home from tending the garden of the 'Big Hoose' at Carskiey . . .

Leaning on our front gate he would observe my potato shaws, puny and raddled by the wind, my bedraggled peas insecurely staked, my small turnips, some of them wooden and running to seed, my carrots wilting under attacks of carrot fly. He would observe Jean's struggling shrubs and sparsely flowering annuals. At the sight he would shut his eyes as if offended and heave a sigh. 'Bloody hell!' he would murmer to himself.

Then, as if confronted with the Holy Grail, he would suddenly become aware of the carnations, red and white, strong and beautiful. And of my bed of parsley. He would shake his head. 'Man,' he would exclaim, in awe, 'is nature no' wunnerfu'! Growin' in poverty!'

GREMLINS IN
MY GARDEN

Angus MacVicar

Confessions of a Harassed Horticulturist

ARROW BOOKS

To Robertson Finlayson,
my gardening guru

Arrow Books Limited
20 Vauxhall Bridge Road, London SW1V 2SA

An imprint of Random Century Group

London Melbourne Sydney Auckland
Johannesburg and agencies throughout
the world

First published by Hutchinson 1985
Arrow edition 1990

Printed and bound in Great Britain by
Courier International Ltd, Tiptree, Essex

ISBN 0 09 969760 2

Contents

1 Through a Glass, Darkly   11
2 Memory Garden   14
3 Faithful Footsteps   27
4 Wise Saws   37
5 And Modern Instances   47
6 Moles at the Mull   61
7 Down to Earth   67
8 As the Swift Seasons Roll   77
9 Interlude: Concerning Alstroemeria   88
10 As the Swift Seasons Roll (continued)   93
11 Satyrs on My Lawn   101
12 Old Wives' Tales   114
13 'A Vegetable Love'   119
14 Rotation   141
15 But Then Face to Face   143

Acknowledgements

For some gardening facts and gardening lore I am indebted to Jean Palaiseul (*Grandmother's Secrets:* Barrie & Jenkins, 1973), to Gail Duff (*Country Wisdom:* Pan Books, 1979), to Christine Kelway (*Gardening on Sand:* W.H. & L. Collingridge, 1965), to David N. Antill (*Home Vegetable Production:* E.P. Publishing, 1976) and to John Seymour (*Gardener's Delight:* Michael Joseph, 1978).

A.M.

1. Through a Glass, Darkly

'The Book of Life,' said Lord Illingworth, 'begins with a man and a woman in a garden.'

'It ends with Revelations,' said Mrs Allonby.

Panting in the wake of Oscar Wilde's literary talent (in *A Woman of No Importance*), I intend to begin with a boy in a garden and to continue with revelations concerning one man's struggle with a garden. A man of no importance, especially in the world of horticulture.

It is probable that professional gardeners will derive no material benefit from such an essay. Neither, I expect, will expert amateurs, who, at a glance, can find meaning in esoteric words and phrases like rotation of crops, the pH scale, legumes, mulching (not to mention leaching), the alkaline factor, humus, brassicas and *campanula poscharskyana*. On the other hand, if they decide to go on reading, they may find themselves laughing, an unusual but possibly therapeutic activity for men and women continually beset by worries concerning frost, gales, blight, canker, caterpillars, slugs, aphids, eelworms, carrot fly and marauding birds and beasts of every description. (*Campanula poscharskyana* is a periwinkle. I looked it up.)

In the main, my revelations are for non-experts like myself: a cry for sympathy, perhaps, on a human rather than a horticultural level.

There is another consideration. Almost every author, fumbling in the dark for readers' minds, from Theophrastus in the third century BC, through Pliny, Bacon, Shakespeare, Culpepper and Kipling down to John Seymour in the present scene, has tried his hand at writing about gardens and the produce of gardens. Why shouldn't I?

This ambition may be compared with that of golfers in all parts of the world who yearn to play with distinction in an Open Championship. I have reached the stage now of wanting to compete alongside the 'greats', even though my garden is little better than a patch of sand above a windy shore at the Mull of Kintyre and my contribution may turn out to be unorthodox and unhelpful to the 'scratch' men among gardeners. I am aware that when describing gardens or offering advice on their management most of my competitors have in mind ideal conditions of both soil and climate. But my garden is not a silk purse. It is the ear of a particularly mangy sow.

I still want to write a gardening book, however, because in spite of the inimical nature of my sand-patch I love it almost as much as I love my golf. (Which is no great shakes either, I may as well confess.) And handicappers like myself may find some stray hint or suggestion in the following pages to comfort and strengthen them in their pursuit of perfection (always vain) in a sweet-smelling rose or a succulent carrot.

Bacon wrote: 'God Almighty first planted a garden; and, indeed, it is the purest of human pleasures.' Thoughts occur to me. Was Francis, in fact, a practical gardener? Or was he merely in love with the idea of a garden?

I am always suspicious of those who insist upon their own moral rectitude and ultimate holiness. In the same way I am suspicious of writers who go on about being 'nearer God's heart in a garden'. Have they ever worked in a garden, their boots clogged with muck, sweat blinding their eyes, muscles aching as they dig and delve, blood pressure rising as they stoop to pluck out burgeoning weeds and thoughts churning savagely as they make passes at the thieving sparrows, burrowing moles and nibbling rabbits? Do they appreciate that a lawn of 'smooth enammell'd green' is often the result of long struggles with a recalcitrant lawn mower, the temperament of whose two-stroke engine is as variable as that of an unbroken colt?

Kipling, I believe, saw 'through a glass, darkly'. In *The Glory of the Garden* he wrote:

Our England is a garden, and such gardens are not made

By singing – 'Oh, how beautiful!' and sitting in the shade,
While better men than we go out and start their working lives
At grubbing weeds from gravel-paths with broken dinner knives.

Despite a peculiar belief, one shared by many of his contemporaries, that England in any respect was superior to all
other countries in the world, Kipling seldom failed to acknow-
ledge that most beautiful things, including gardens and the
British Empire, were the result of hard and unremitting
labour, 'under the mid-day sun' if need be. And his reference
to 'broken dinner knives' is proof that his sympathies –
though perhaps in a vague poetic blur – lay with the under-
privileged who could not afford to employ a gardener or,
indeed, a butler to maintain the condition of their cutlery.

In the same poem he made the significant observation that
'half a proper gardener's work is done upon his knees'. He
meant this metaphorically as well as literally, of course, and
well he might. When I am not praying for rain for my garden, I
am praying for a cessation of the gales which frequently blow
over my native parish of Southend. If, by some happy chance,
the rains come and the gales blow themselves out, I pray for
sunshine. And when the sunshine sparkles and warm air from
the Gulf Stream bears down upon my arid soil I pray for rain
again.

Golfers are never fully satisfied with their efforts. Neither
are authors. Neither are farmers and multimillionaires. (There
is a difference.) And neither are gardeners. But then, in this
game of life, is anyone ever fully satisfied? Who – apart, it
may be, from the Pope, the Archbishop of Canterbury and the
Director General of the BBC – who, I ask, has found the
Holy Grail? Nevertheless, the search is fascinating, funny and
exciting. It is my main excuse for writing about it.

2. Memory Garden

In 1910 my father became the Church of Scotland minister of Southend at the Mull of Kintyre. He and my mother found themselves installed in a manse containing a dining room and drawing room, five bedrooms, a kitchen, a scullery (twice the size of any modern kitchen) and a bathroom. Adjoining it, a legacy from the days when the minister farmed the glebe-lands, were stables, byres and other outhouses, including an earthen closet. The manse and its auxiliary buildings stood in about an acre and a half of garden.

The ministerial annual stipend was £180, out of which my parents were able, at first, to afford two maids. One of them was Jessie MacLaren from Perthshire, who, eventually, came near to ousting my father as dictator of this small kingdom. Five feet nothing of flashing temper, hard knuckles and implacable discipline, she was always known in the family – for what reason I never discovered – as 'Maimie'.

At this point it may be useful to remind readers south of the Border that the Church of Scotland, the national Church, is not to be confused with the Free Church of Scotland or the Free Presbyterian Church of Scotland. The Church of Scotland is by no means thirled to doom and gloom and negative virtues, as Jean Rook and other Sassenach journalists appear to believe. Many of its members, elders and ministers, while attending faithfully to their duties, both moral and material, lead reasonably normal lives. They enjoy their card games and their golf, their football and their shinty. And their wee dram, even on a Sunday. They are much more understanding and tolerant than any Fleet Street gossiper.

At the time of the Rev. Angus J. MacVicar's induction to the parish of Southend I was eighteen months old. As the years went by the family increased. Archie and Willie were born before World War I, during which my father served as a padre with the Lovat Scouts, for a time in Salonika. Afterwards, in the parish, he was always known as 'the Padre'. Rona, Kenneth and John all put in an appearance after the war, John being nineteen years younger than I.

The manse garden was our childhood playground. Perhaps we failed to appreciate it fully when we were young, but now, more than half a century on, those of us who are still alive understand how privileged we were to have it.

At the front was a huge lawn surrounded by plane and ash trees, interspersed with laburnum and rhododendron bushes. In the middle of the lawn, which was shaggy and seldom mown, there stood a giant copper beech, with a stout branch twelve feet above the ground convenient for a swing. From an ornate iron gate a gravelled avenue led round the lawn to the front door.

At the back were the currant bushes, the apple trees, the holly trees, the flower beds and three large vegetable patches. The soil here was dark and rich, having been cultivated with care by a succession of ministers (or, more likely, their beadles) for over a hundred years. Until my father began operations I am sure no artificial fertilizer had ever been applied to it. A yearly scattering of dung from the midden at the back, always kept full by the horses and cattle which inhabited the glebe in summer and the stable and byres in winter, was enough to keep it in good heart.

For the sake of delicately nurtured readers I hesitate to mention that human excrement from the outside dry closet was also used in abundance. But I do so in the knowledge that gardeners who actually garden – as opposed to those who only write poetically about gardens – have come to realize that beauty of appearance, taste or smell often springs from what the world deems crudity. (Is there a moral here somewhere?)

The Padre was not a dedicated gardener. As the descendant of a long line of crofters in North Uist, however, he had the earth in his blood. On vacations from school and university he had often taken part in the digging, drying and stacking of peats. And in the preparation of 'lazy-beds' for potatoes.

In the Highlands and Islands of Scotland the 'lazy-bed' method of growing potatoes was used until about the end of last century. It consisted of laying the seed on the surface and then covering it with earth from trenches dug along both sides. In the machars of the Outer Hebrides and on many a hillside in Argyll traces of the 'lazy-beds' can still be seen, especially in aerial photographs. Deep grassy ruts in the middle of the 13th fairway of Dunaverty Golf Course, which cause even scratch men to utter wails of anguish, are an example.

The Padre was also a skilled and enthusiastic shinty player, the result being that for a clergyman his arms and wrists were unusually strong. As, on occasions, we bent over the piano stool to receive punishment for a misdemeanor, we were provided with convincing evidence of this.

In accordance with his Hebridean temperament, which, it has to be said, I have inherited, he was, however, inclined to accomplish any physical tasks in sudden, desperate bursts of energy. Presently this energy would wane. Urgent matters of the spirit, such as the thinking out of a sermon in his slippers by the fire, would engage his attention, and his wife and children would receive sharp orders to complete the work.

But there is no doubt that when he attacked the garden he did so with effect. In his shirtsleeves and with 'gallowses' dangling – but still wearing his dog collar – he could dig up a vegetable patch with as much efficiency and speed as any labouring man. In the course of such activity his ordinarily ruddy face would become ruddier still, and his neck would bulge over his collar. His volatile temper would rise towards flash point and we, as children, always tended to avoid the garden when he was working in it.

Our absence, however, was often an added irritation to him. Sometimes he would thrust the spade into the ground with violence and come stomping round to the front of the house.

'Where are those boys?' he would demand of the sky, as if expecting an answer from the Almighty. 'Where are those lazy, skulking boys, who leave me to do everything myself?'

From the shelter of the thick hedge which separated the Manse grounds from a field belonging to Donald Galbraith, the neighbouring farmer, we would remain still, listening and watching.

Maimie would erupt from the scullery, flourishing a dish-cloth. She, too, had rhetorical questions to ask. 'Poor boys, can't they be left alone, even on a Saturday? *Chiall beannachd mi*, isn't it enough for one person to get his boots dirty for me to clean?'

The Padre would ignore her. 'Mama!' he would shout. 'Mama, where are you?'

My mother would appear, hands floury from baking, smiling and calm. 'Yes, Dada. What's worrying you?'

'What's worrying me? I'm trying to get the garden done, and I still have to write a sermon for tomorrow, and nobody' – suddenly the angry tone would become almost pitiful – 'nobody will help me. Where are those blasted boys?'

'Wherever they are,' Maimie would mutter, 'they're a lot happier than they would be here!'

My mother knew exactly where we were, but her mission in life was to keep peace at the manse, which, with the Padre and Maimie around, was a task that might have daunted even Mother Teresa. Quickly forestalling further acrimony between her husband and her maid, she would say: 'I think you've done enough this morning, dear. Why don't you go inside now and start your sermon. Maimie and I will find the boys and get them to finish the digging.'

'Maybe you're right, Mama. But those boys need more discipline! Why are they never here when I want them?'

Then he would proceed indoors, with Maimie, only slightly out of earshot, complaining at his back: 'And take off those dirty boots in the scullery. I don't want my kitchen looking like a midden!'

Later in the day my mother would collect us. 'We'll finish the digging for Dada,' she would say. 'Poor Dada, he has so much to do. Christenings and funerals and weddings and visitations and his sermon for Sunday. He'll be so pleased if we can help him in the garden. One reason we're in this world at all is to help others.'

We were inclined to be rebellious. The young always are, I think, when subjected to subtle attacks of moral guidance. But we did our best to finish the digging, mainly because it distressed us to see our mother trying to do it, in a 'hobble' skirt which seemed to cling tightly round her ankles. Digging, we were convinced, was no job for a frail woman. (In fact, our mother was anything but frail. But she *was* our mother.)

We were well aware, however, that when the Padre, having completed his sermon, came to inspect our work, he would condemn it as being utterly useless. 'A spell at the peats would do you all a lot of good!'

At such an early age we were, indeed, fairly useless in the garden, not only on account of our puny muscles but also because we had no interest in it whatsoever except as a splendid playground and as a source of tasty fruits and vegetables.

When our mates from the village and the surrounding farms, both male and female, came to the manse on a summer evening to play Smuggle the Keg, Cowboys and Indians and other rough games – the rougher the more enjoyable, even for the girls – our favourite hiding places were among the rows of green peas and sticks of rhubarb, below the gooseberry and currant bushes and in the branches of the twin apple trees. Succulent peas and fruit could be consumed at leisure, excitement honing already keen appetites. When the chase was on we trampled through the garden, regardless of damage, and at the end of the evening the girls' dresses would be torn, boys' trousers ripped above bleeding knees and the garden left as if stricken by a typhoon.

If such a thing happened in my garden today and my vegetables were purloined and eaten by marauders I should be inclined to call on God, Auld Nick and perhaps even the police to administer vengeance. Strangely, the Padre seldom made more than a token remonstrance. It was Maimie who would run about like an enraged bantam, uttering threats in the Gaelic.

'Your poor father, working his fingers to the bone to have a nice garden, and now you go and ruin it!'

'Look out, Maimie, there's an Indian at your back with a bow and arrow!'

'Ach, I'll put the Indian sign on *him*!' She would pick up a graip or a rake and make swipes at the unfortunate boy.

'Get out of here, you young rascal, and play somewhere else!'

Once I was astonished to hear the Padre, who had appeared from his study wearing a shabby old cardigan – and his dog collar – making soothing sounds to her. 'Och, leave them alone, Maimie. They're enjoying themselves.'

It was as if Jack Dempsey, the Manassa Mauler, had stopped in the middle of a fight to smile and pat his opponent's head. It made me feel uneasy, almost guilty. Next day, if it was fine, we sometimes went out and did our best to tidy up the peas and the rhubarb and the currant bushes. And we would sample the produce once again, just to verify that no real harm had come to it.

When we grew up and were out and about in the world, with families of our own, the manse garden remained a source of adventure for boys in the parish. Children no longer played in it, but after dark on autumn evenings exciting raids could be carried out, the main targets being the gooseberry bushes and the apple trees. Rumour had it that the old minister could be pretty fierce, which added spice to the forays. Cool calculation, however, pointed to the fact that even though he did emerge unexpectedly on the scene his rheumaticky legs would make it difficult for him to catch them; and in the dark, without his half-moon spectacles, he would certainly be unable to identify them.

Late one September evening, while reading in his study – possibly a book by the Australian clergyman, F.W. Boreham, who provided ministers all over the world with apt 'illustrations' for sermons – he decided to go outside for a breath of air. He also wanted to have a look at the new moon and flip over the sixpenny pieces in his pocket. (To a Hebridean, like my father, though he often thundered against superstition from the pulpit, it was unlucky to see a new moon for the first time through glass. On the other hand, if he saw it bare and plain, at the same time turning over a silver coin, it brought good luck in the coming month.)

As he went through the ritual he heard scuffling sounds and glimpsed shadows moving out of the garden and over the wall. Quickly he padded round to the yard. Nobody was to be seen. There was a steep bank on the other side of the main road covered with bushes and trees where an army platoon could lie hidden and secure. But at the door of the byre near the road he saw moonlight glinting on metal. Propped against the wall he found a boy's bicycle, brand new. And he knew whose bicycle it was. Young Sammy's. From the Argyll Arms, which we called The Inn.

He wheeled the bicycle into the manse and parked it in the scullery. Then he went out into the garden and, with a torch, discovered a small bag half-filled with apples, discarded at the foot of one of the trees. He brought that indoors, too.

In the morning my mother and Maimie found him in a mood of the utmost amiability. He explained what had happened and chuckled in a less than holy way. 'Sooner or later Sammy will have to come for his new bike and confess his crime. I just want to see how he handles it. You remember Shakespeare, Maimie? "For 'tis the sport to have the engineer hoist with his own petar" '.

'Ach, Shakespeare! There's a better saying in the Gaelic. "*Tha e grunnachadh na eabar fhein.*" (Falling in his own mud.)' But she approved the Padre's arrangements, even though it meant that for a time her scullery would be cluttered up with the bicycle and the bag of apples.

My mother said: 'Poor Sammy!' And smiled.

The days passed. The strain on Sammy must have been considerable. His new bike had been the joy of his heart and the envy of his mates in the village. Now he had to watch them pedalling past him to school, while he was forced to walk, slowly and sadly, their shouts of derision adding to his burden. His reputation as a daring 'apple raider' had sunk to a shameful level.

One day, while having lunch, my father observed from the window of the dining room a chubby, blond-haired boy lingering at the front gate.

'Look, Mama, here's Sammy trying to make up his mind to come in!'

'Well, I hope he does come in. Poor Sammy!'

The gate opened and Sammy came up the avenue, head low, footsteps dragging. The doorbell rang.

'I'll go,' said my mother.

'No, indeed. You'd be much too soft with him.'

Sammy raised his eyes from the front doorstep – newly patterned by Maimie with whorls of white pipe-clay – and saw the Padre looming above him.

'Yes, Sammy?'

'Can – can I have my bike?'

'Oh, was that your bike I found about a week ago, at the byre door?'

'Ay.'

'How on earth did it come to be there?'

There was a silence. Then, showing courage far finer than any ordinary 'apple raider', Sammy said: 'We – we were – we were stealing your apples.'

'Dear me, Sammy. Don't you know that stealing is a sin?'

'Ay.'

'Are you sorry for what you were doing?'

'Ay.'

'But even sorrier that you lost your bike?'

'Ay.'

For the life of him the Padre could summon up no anger, real or spurious. 'Well,' he said, 'your bike's in the scullery. Come and get it.'

Sammy's eyes shone as he began to wheel it outside, even though Maimie was behind him, scolding and calling him a 'young rascal' and a disgrace to his parents.

'You've forgotten something,' said the Padre.

Sammy paused.

'Here's your bag of apples. Go out to the garden and fill it before you go. Share them with your friends.'

Maimie broke into a long Gaelic imprecation which consigned the Padre to the devil for his week-kneed response to criminal behaviour.

Sammy was speechless. He took the bag, went into the garden as he had been told and put a few more apples into the bag. But he took his bike with him and kept a wary eye on it – and on the Padre – all the time.

As eventually he disappeared round the corner at the kirk, the bag of apples tied to his handlebars, his back was straight; he was pedalling fast and whistling a happy tune.

Said the Padre: 'Remember the Gaelic proverb, Maimie. A stick from the wood, a deer from the hill and a salmon from the burn, the prerogative of every true Highlander. To which may be added apples from the manse garden.'

Maimie shook her head, made a sneering sound and went back to the dishes at the sink.

My mother came with more dishes from the dining room. 'I hope neither of you were too hard on Sammy,' she said, without, like Pilate, staying for an answer. 'Now,' she directed the Padre, 'go and have your snooze until the Guild ladies arrive.'

The garden was surrounded by trees: plane, ash, beech (including the copper beech with the swing) and one huge spreading chestnut. Today many of them have been cut down because of age and deteriorating condition. The high branches gave shelter to many birds, raucous crows among them. Blackbirds lived among the lower foliage, making summer mornings sweet with their singing. At certain seasons thrushes, robins, tits, finches and wagtails played tag with cheeky sparrows on the grass below.

In our imagination the thick undergrowth around their roots was the lair of lions, tigers and other dangerous animals. Sometimes, in wintry weather, it was indeed inhabited, by pheasants from the hill seeking shelter. We were not afraid of them. We trapped them for the pot, using a special method of our own. But that is another story.

At about the midway stage of his long ministry in Southend – he retired in 1957 – the Padre filled the back garden with a number of more exotic trees, such as Japanese larch and ornamental firs. They provided shelter for the vegetable garden. They also covered more than a quarter of an acre of ground which he no longer had to dig.

The new plantation contained a single palm which became, in time, the home of a large brown owl. On a moonlit night, when we felt in need of excitement, we would creep out into the garden and, from a safe distance, stare up at the baleful eyes staring back down at us from among the fronds. Shivers of terror, which were also pleasurable, would invade our muscles.

The sight of our flourishing palm used to astonish visitors from England who believed that the Mull of Kintyre, wild and rugged, could never sustain a tree of tropical descent. But the Padre would point out that the Gulf Stream passed nearby, providing the whole west coast of Scotland with a mild and beneficial climate seldom vitiated by frosts. In any case, the palm existed in a surrounding shelter of evergreens.

As proof of the balminess of the Hebridean air he would also refer to the fact that every year certain rare plants used to be sent from Kew Gardens in London to winter in the open at Inverewe in Wester Ross, which is more than 150 miles farther north than the Mull of Kintyre. (The Mull is on the same latitude as Alnwick in Northumberland. Our flowers and vegetables can be sown and planted at least a month earlier than in the north and east of Scotland.)

The palm tree in the manse garden still exists, ancient and somewhat decrepit. Only once have I known it to flower. It happened not long before my mother died in 1963.

When the Padre became old and mystical – he died in 1970 at the age of ninety-two – he would often tell us about the Gaelic paradise of *Tir nan Og*, the land of the ever young beyond the western sea, 'where the souls of the departed find rest and peace'. Then his eyes would become keen and even calculating. 'Did it ever occur to you boys' – we were boys to him, even though some of us were bordering sixty – 'did it ever occur to you that *Tir nan Og* may be a folk memory of Atlantis? Atlantis, out there in the west, where the climate was subtropical and rare plants grew in profusion. Like the palm tree in the garden.' Then the eyes would become cloudy again. 'Could the mildness we enjoy here in the west be a legacy from that lost land? The land of our forefathers . . .'

More than two thousand years ago Plato described the condition of Atlantis:

There was abundant grazing, not only for all the animals that live in swamps, ponds, lakes, as well as on the mountains and the plains. . . . The island also grew and amply provided all the aromatic substances, roots, trees, herbs and various gums exuded by flowers and fruit. There were bananas and cereals that provide our staple diet, pulse which is also needed to sustain us. There were fruit-bearing trees that yielded drink, food and oil but are perishable; they are grown for our delectation and pleasure after meals as a welcome stimulant to the sated palate. All this the island, which was bathed in sunshine, divine, beautiful and a wonder to behold, produced in superb quality and immeasurable abundance.

I think that Plato's vision was similar to that of the Padre. And, indeed, to that of the writer of the Book of Genesis. They all imagined paradise to exist in a garden full of fertility. The search for it is instinctive in all humanity. That we cannot quite reach it in this life is no cause for despair. Some day, somewhere we shall find it.

Our small ricketty carrots will look like colour advertisements. Our scabby potatoes will be smooth, egg-shaped and firm. Our leeks will be like pillars of white marble and our frothing roses will exude the scent of happiness.

It is a long time since five boys and one little girl played with their friends in the manse garden.

Archie and Rona did not live long enough to enjoy gardens of their own.

With an honours degree in English, Archie became a schoolteacher. He married his Mima and set up house in Dunoon. Soon afterwards World War II cut a black swathe, like acid rain, through the young and hopeful. He did not escape. He was killed in Sicily in July 1943, during an attack by the Argylls across the plain of Gerbini.

Like Archie, Rona became a schoolteacher. She died of cancer in 1949, not long after winning the Gold Medal for solo singing at the Gaelic Mod in Glasgow. Her favourite plant in the manse garden was the southernwood. Its old fashioned scent was always in her room. I still have a book she gave me, with the chapter she wanted me to read marked by a few dry, dead sprigs of it.

But Willie, Kenneth, John and I still survive.

John, the youngest – and too young to have taken part in the war – became a doctor. He is now Professor of Midwifery at Leicester University. I often wonder why it is that the most youthful member of almost every MacVicar family is the cleverest. In John's case, however, this does not apply in a horticultural sense. His patient wife, Esmé, produces the flowers and the fruit in their garden, while he concentrates on producing babies at his hospital.

Willie served for many years as a ship's captain with the Anchor Line. During the war, with others, he spent twenty-one days in an open lifeboat, after the sinking of the *Britannia* off the northwest coast of Africa. Eventually he and his fellow survivors landed in Brazil. Some years ago, somewhat reluctantly, he retired to tend the garden of his house in Troon. He considers himself to be an expert gardener, having been tutored by his wife, Nina, and by his father-in-law who actually won prizes at horticultural shows. When I try to discuss points of detail with him, such as the relative merits of Bromophos and Gamma BHC for carrot fly, he is inclined to laugh at me in a pitying way.

Kenneth has been minister of Kenmore in Perthshire since 1950 and is now known to irreverent colleagues as the Bishop of Loch Tayside. In 1944, while piloting a Hurricane in Burma, he was shot down. He spent a week in the jungle, dodging the Japanese, before being arrested as a vagabond by a company of the Gordon Highlanders.

The grounds of the Kenmore manse are even more extensive than those of the manse in Southend. But the soil in the garden is rich and fertile: so rich and fertile, indeed, that if left to itself it would soon produce a jungle as thick as one in Burma. Sometimes, when Kenneth has been busier than usual with parish work – and, it must be admitted, games of golf – it threatens to do so, great Triffid growths looming up around the raspberry canes and the apple trees.

At this point the Bishop of Loch Tayside abandons prayer and becomes practical. His wife, Isobel, his daughter, Jean, and his sons, Angus, Kenneth and Cameron, are all summoned to his aid, along with workers press-ganged from amongst the congregation. In several days of unremitting toil (and of imprecations unsuited to an environment touched by holiness) the Triffids are attacked and repulsed, and wonderful crops of potatoes, strawberries and vegetables of all descriptions burgeon in the cleansed ground.

Kenneth, however, does take a continuing interest in his garden, unlike a neighbour of mine who plays golf and chess during the long months of winter and spring and then, at about the beginning of June, calls upon all his friends to assist him in what he describes as his 'garden day'.

Starting at six o'clock in the morning, with early sunshine winking on the grass, they clear the ground, spread dung upon it, dig it, rake it, sow seeds of both flowers and vegetables, plant potatoes, cabbages and cauliflowers, leeks and lettuce, prune the roses, run a Flymo over his tiny lawn and make a bonfire of all the waste material.

While this is going on, my neighbour, who is, admittedly, of advanced years, moves around among the chain gang, hospitably ministering to their needs in regard to food and drink and praising their efforts in a fulsome and irritating way.

By dusk the task is done. Then, with declarations of undying gratitude chuntering in their ears, the workers return to their homes and dear ones, exhausted and wondering how, year after year, they succumb so easily to my neighbour's guileful charm.

To the chagrin of many, from June to September, his garden is by far the most successful and admired in the district.

Archie and Rona often told me how, in times of anxiety and fear, the memory of the manse garden came to comfort them. Willie, Kenneth, John and I remember it, too, and put into practice many of the hard lessons, both spiritual and physical, which we learned in it from our parents.

My own sandy ground has been fortified by tons of rich, dark soil taken from it during a recent excavation, when a car park was built outside the manse back door. But my cabbages are still not as large and beautiful as the ones my father used to grow.

3. Faithful Footsteps

Jean and I were married on 24 June 1936. The Padre conducted the service in the Kirk of St Blaan, Southend. He was assisted by the Rev. Kenneth MacLeod, who wrote the words of the internationally famous song, 'The Road to the Isles'.

Kenneth's mother was a Cornishwoman, his father a native of Skye. The combination bequeathed to him an alert, somewhat wry expression, sallow skin and glistening brown eyes. According to himself, these were the characteristics of the original 'small dark men' who, in the dark millennia before the coming of Christ, found their way into the British Isles from the Mediterranean (and territories even farther to the east) and are loosely labelled 'Celts'.

Like my father, who was blond and ready to admit that he owed his fair colouring to Scandinavian ancestors marauding among the Celts of the Outer Hebrides, Kenneth was superstitious. 'We may call ourselves Presbyterian ministers,' he used to chuckle to my father, 'but you and I, Angus, we're one third Protestant, one third Catholic and one third pagan.'

As a boy in my early teens I was present on the day Kenneth was inducted minister of the island of Gigha, a few miles off the west coast of Kintyre. (The story is that Gigha means 'God's island'; and, indeed, it seems to get more than its fair share of sunshine. But Gaelic scholars agree that the name probably comes from the Gaelic word *I*, which means, simply, 'an island'.) After the service Kenneth insisted upon planting two rowan trees, one on each side of the gate leading from the road to the new church. 'To keep away the fairies,' he said, not entirely as an example of Celtic humour.

Those rowan trees still flourish. I have a cutting from one of them growing near the left-hand pillar of my own garden gate.

When Jean and I are translated to *Tir nan Og* – as I hope we shall be, later rather than sooner – our son Jock may take a cutting from it and plant it near the right-hand pillar, thus completing the circle in the traditional Celtic manner, from left to right.

No true Celt would ever contemplate working from right to left. That would be doing it 'widdershins', the devil's way, and bad luck would surely follow. In AD 562 before St Columba led his men into battle against Diarmit at Culdreimnhe, he marched his men sunwise around the sacred cairn, in accordance with Druidical rites. He won the day. And I have always believed that what was good enough for Columba is good enough for me. For example, I would never dream of putting on my left sock first. Or for that matter, my left shoe, especially if I were about to golf or garden.

All this may seem strange to readers of Anglo-Saxon origin, untainted – as they believe – by Celtic mysticism. But are they so untainted? When digging their gardens, don't they work from left to right? When dibbling in their leek plants in May or June, don't they do the same?

Come to think of it, I may try planting another rowan cutting myself. It might help to counter, more successfully than netting wire and unsightly planks of wood under the gate, the attacks of young rabbits upon my unfortunate vegetables.

While Jean and I were on our honeymoon, the finishing touches were being given to the bungalow we had built above the shore, a mile and a half down the road from the manse and the kirk. We had called it Achnamara, a sweet sounding Gaelic name which means, prosaically, 'the field by the sea'. The size of our field was a quarter of an acre.

We live there still, like Shakespeare's Timon, in our 'everlasting mansion upon the beached verge of the salt flood'.

Behind us steep escarpments mark the remains of two raised beaches. They give us a hint of shelter from a nor'west wind. Both are clad thickly in whins, which, if the weather remains mild, can go on flowering all the year round. The travelling people at the Mull of Kintyre have a saying: 'A time for kissing when the whin's in bloom.' I wish some of our modern, 'sophisticated' politicians could appreciate the smile in their eyes as they repeat it.

On a clear day, seventeen miles to the sou'west, we can see the hills of Antrim rising improbably into the sky, like a backdrop in a Walt Disney film. Across the bay from our front door there looms the squat, green rock of Dunaverty, with the remains of a MacDonald castle on its summit.

In 1647 a Covenanting army under General Leslie, reinforced by the fighting levies of *Gillesbuig Gruamach* – otherwise Archibald of the Twisted Mouth, Marquis of Argyll – besieged Dunaverty. In the end they burned the castle and massacred its garrison. The fire marks are still visible on the ancient stones. Today the normal tranquillity of the Rock gives no hint of its cruel history; but when a gale screams in from the south and heavy waves burst against it, spume flying high, then we hear the Hammers of Fingal and are reminded of the violence and terror of the old days.

The hammering sound occurs in a cave near the river mouth, under the shadow of the Rock. Long ago a local schoolboy, pondering a Celtic legend, wrote verses about it.

> The rushing rattle of wave upon wave
>   Comes echoing out like a crackle of guns
> As the sea-swell lifts and assaults the cave;
>   And the song of the smith through the roaring runs:
>   'Doom will sound ere we are free
>   (Wield them, *gillean*, keep your pledges!)
>   Till no motion stirs the sea
>   Hissing forges feed the sledges.'
>
> In murky gloom, when the storm king rides,
>   The smith and his men work all night long;
> The hammers crash on the anvil sides,
>   And loud 'mid the din is the blacksmith's song:
>   'Fingal's armour shape once more.
>   (Wield them *gillean*: keep your pledges!)
>   Work is hard when tempests roar;
>   Glowing forges feed the sledges.'
>
> The waters are calm and the winds die;
>   Slowly the ripples slide o'er the shingle;

> In the cave is a patter and murm'ring sigh,
>   And the song of the smith and the wavelets mingle:
>   'Ullin's harp-frame weld again.
>   (Softly, *gillean*: keep your pledges!)
>   Ease your bodies, ease your pain;
>   Dim the forge, lay by the sledges.'

The usual way of access to the Roaring Cave, as we call it, is by boat from the sea. But sometimes at low tide, when we were boys, we were able to scramble round on slippery rocks and look into it. There was always a rustle and a patter in the dark interior and occasionally an alarming rattle of wings as rock pigeons flew out at us. We never failed to experience a thrill of terror, which was what we had come for; and we never wasted a moment in scurrying back to the firm ground at the river mouth. 'In case the tide comes in,' we told one another. But it wasn't the tide of which we were scared.

Despatches from General Leslie tell us that a number of MacDonald soldiers from the garrison were able to hide in this cave for a time and thus escape the massacre. Eventually, however, they were 'smok'd out like foxes' and sent as slave labour to France. A few came back, among them a young lad called McCoig. He was an ancestor of Jean's. (When I do something to displease Jean, such as coming in from the garden with dung on my boots, and she becomes coldly inimical, I sometimes tell her that I wish young McCoig had stayed in France. This does nothing to sweeten the occasion.)

All this mixture of legend and history stirs my imagination. That is, when a romantic mood is on me. When I feel more practical, I am equally interested in a deep cleft in the rock front between the Roaring Cave and the river mouth. Known locally as the Stinking Hole, it is a receptacle for seaweed thrown in by high tides and storms; seaweed which, if not removed by succeeding high tides and storms, lies rotting in the sun, causing a prodigious stench.

Fifty years ago, when farmers had to depend upon natural fertilizers rather than on mixtures produced by scientists, much of this used to be carted and spread on the fields. Nowadays no one puts any value on it except a few gardeners who are instinctively wary of using too many 'artificials', myself among them.

I carry the seaweed home in bags slung across my back. Sometimes this triggers off an attack of fibrositis in my neck muscles. But what is a small pain here or there in the establishment of good, rich soil?

It has also been the cause of some mild embarrassment to Jean. One afternoon, not long ago, she was entertaining a stylish friend of hers in the 'good room' when I happened to come up from the shore carrying a dripping sackful of seaweed. The stylish lady, seated by the window, glimpsed me coming in by the front gate. My jerkin was ancient and torn; my patched trousers were tucked into wellington boots.

'Oh, my dear, have you engaged a gardener? What a villainous looking creature!'

Jean took a double take, then smiled her most confidential smile. 'No, no. Just an old tinker who comes looking for a job. Do have some more tea.'

But I must return to a description of our 'field by the sea'.

Jean and I remain slightly bemused by the fact that the house, garage and a surrounding concrete wall cost only £1000, £600 of which we borrowed from the Argyll County Council. Today the insurance value of the place is forty times that amount. The loan was paid off many years ago; and the ground, originally feu-ed, now belongs to us. If the oilmen come – as they will – planting their skeletal rigs in the blue waters of the Firth of Clyde or the North Channel and demanding shore-room which will obliterate Achnamara, we will man the barricades and fight them to the last.

This quarter of an acre of ours, though continually assaulted by rains, winds and flying spray, now has the appearance of a garden, with small trees and bushes peeping gingerly above the shelter of the wall. When Jean and I returned from our honeymoon, however, the place was a daunting sight. Its green surface was trampled and torn by the builders and their vehicles, and bricks, large stones and rubble lay everywhere in lumps.

To my aid came my brothers Archie and Kenneth – by this time Willie was at sea with the Anchor Line – and Jean's brothers James and Peter, who were farming at her old home, Brunerican, on the other side of the golf course. (I had made sure that my future home should be less than two good drives and a long iron from the first tee.) We aimed to complete the work of shaping the ground and the garden in a single operation, and – luckily as we thought – the appointed day was warm and sunny, with only a whisper of wind and a darkening western horizon.

Archie, Kenneth, James and I laboured to rid the ground of the rocks and rubble. When this was done we began to dig the garden patches at the rear of the house and the lawn in front. Meanwhile, Peter, with a bored looking Clydesdale mare and a single furrow plough, carefully scraped away about nine inches of turf and topsoil to form a broad track from the front gate to the garage door.

Later, I spread along this 'avenue's' length a few tons of gravel from the beach. Some fifty years on, the same gravel still lies there, because the bottom is so rock hard that it cannot sink into it.

Having dug the lawn, we then used the soil and turf from the 'avenue' – laying the turf grass-side down – to build a small terrace rising up from it to the flower-plots and narrow path in front of the house. We shaped it tenderly, rounding its ends. With turf left over we lined the edges of the 'avenue'.

Finally, I sowed grass seed on the lawn, while Archie rolled it with a small roller I had borrowed from a neighbour.

At about seven o'clock in the evening, as the wind began to rise and storm clouds came looming up over the Mull, we decided to call it a day and sat down to a large meal prepared by Jean. One of the courses was vegetable broth, which is my favourite of all soups, as long as it contains a dash of tomato and plenty of green peas. Spooning it up with relish, I vowed to myself that some day I would grow in my garden all the necessary ingredients, especially the peas.

After the meal we had a dram and enjoyed a *ceilidh* in our new 'good room', with Jean at the piano. Rona, who had been helping Jean with the catering arrangements, did most of the singing. (The old mare, having consumed a tasty bag of oats, stood somnolently outside the garage door, no doubt

wondering what all the noise was about.) By the time everybody went home a gale from the south was blowing and rain,
mingled with spray whipped up from the sea, was splashing on
the windows.

Next morning, when I got up and looked out, I found that
during the night the storm had blown most of the grass seed
off the lawn and flung it in a sullen heap against the front
door. Later in the day, with an anxious heart, I sowed the lawn
all over again, hoping that when growth did come it would not
prove to be too patchy. My hope was vain. It took several
years of amateur experiment before I achieved an even spread
of grass.

My first experience as a gardener in my own right taught
me that when seed is to be sown a careful eye must be kept
upon the weather. 'Wait for the tid,' is the advice given by our
local farmers, 'tid' meaning simply 'tide' (in relation to the
weather) or 'opportunity'.

As a beginner, I thought gardening would prove to be easy,
in much the same way as I had imagined, at first, that writing books would be easy. After all, the ground on which
Achnamara stood was not far from the cemetery at Keil, part
of which, until room had to be found for corpses rather than
for cabbages, had flourished as a garden since the time of St
Columba, fourteen hundred years ago. My soil was similar.
Why then shouldn't it produce flowers and vegetables as
readily as the Keil soil had done?

'St Columba's Footprints' are incised on a flat rock over-
looking the cemetery. The left foot points to the north, the
right foot (size eight, as it happens) to the east. They are the
focus of a legend.

When Columba was exiled from Ireland in AD 563 for
having caused the deaths of three thousand of King Diarmit's
men at the Battle of Culdreimnhe, he and his disciples are said
to have grounded their coracle first at Keil, the nearest land-
fall, before going on to Iona. There, standing on the rock, he
preached the first Christian sermon to his kinsfolk in the Scots
tribe of the *Epidii*, building a new faith on the foundations of
an old pagan one. The 'footstep' pointing east, towards the

rising sun, had been in existence for at least six hundred years before his arrival, being one of the many Druidical 'fealty feet' used in Ireland and Scotland by chiefs swearing faithfulness to their tribes or clans.

I stood in the footsteps and looked down at the cemetery where the old garden had been. In imagination I saw Columba and his disciples, with their crude implements, digging and sowing and harvesting the same ground. Columba had gone, leaving only a small cross cut in the stone above the holy well. The people and the houses had gone, too, leaving only faint traces of an old road and even older foundation stones. But the ground was still there, lush and green, though unfortunately now covered with gravestones rather than with 'bourtrie' (elderberries) and kale. (To the rocks above the holy well cling branches of an ancient ivy. Around it watercress still grows.)

Columba had started a garden which had flourished. And what Columba could do, so might I. Words would flow and books would follow. So I thought. I was only vaguely conscious of the fact that books and gardens need a great deal of planning and devoted labour – and strength of spirit to counter disappointment – before they appear in full glory.

In our three years at Achnamara preceding the outbreak of World War II, Jean and I had only a secondary eye on the garden. Jock was born and required attention, for a time at all hours of the day and night. (He remains intent upon making his voice heard loudly, but now this happens only on the radio or in the columns of the *Daily Express*, about golf and football.) I had a precarious but exciting living to earn as a freelance author which entailed much thought, organization and dedication to my pen and typewriter. And, in spare moments, there was the golf. The garden was low on our list of priorities.

We did indeed plant bushes in what we reckoned were fairly sheltered places – veronicas, fuchsias, flowering currants, hydrangeas, which were varieties recommended for sandy ground by my mother, no slouch as a gardener when allowed by the Padre to operate as one. In due course they took root. We planted climbing roses on either side of the front door and, *mirabile dictu*, one of them is still there: a Paul Scarlet, hoary with age like ourselves but also full of vigour. (In a sunny summer it cascades down the cream coloured wall in dazzling red.)

In narrow plots around the house and walls Jean planted carnations, aubrietias, poppies, primroses, daffodils, crocuses and snowdrops as permanent inhabitants, each year sowing in addition such annuals as took her fancy. For my part I dug the vegetable garden faithfully every spring, planted potatoes, sowed peas, turnips, carrots, lettuce and parsley. In our ignorance we used no fertilizers, expecting God and the ground to do the rest.

In the first year or two, because the ground had lain fallow for some time, the results were fair.

Jean's carnations were a triumph: we had no idea why. Only much later did we realize that our sandy, acid soil was ideal for their propagation.

For me, parsley grew well. (My golfing friend, Big Allan, often reminds me – when I beat him, which is not all that often – of an old belief that parsley grows better for a wicked man than for a good one. 'Didn't you know,' he once said, 'that before germinating, it goes seven times down to the devil and back?' It's a thought. It does take an unconscionable time to 'braird'. About as long as Big Allan takes to size up a putt.) Parsley is supposed to need plenty of humus. At the beginning humus was exactly what the Achnamara garden lacked. But still, for some mysterious reason, my parsley was a fair match, in terms of success, for Jean's carnations.

Old Alec, our friend and neighbour, used to stop and talk to us as he cycled home from tending the garden of the 'Big Hoose' at Carskiey.

He had been a soldier in World War I and, according to his story, had been 'over the top', with bayonet fixed, no less than six times. On the last occasion he had been severely wounded by an exploding shell, part of his jaw being destroyed. He spoke with a nasal intonation, no doubt due to the fact that he now possessed what he proudly called a 'silver ja' '. Leaning on our front gate he would observe my potato shaws, puny and raddled by the wind, my bedraggled peas insecurely staked, my small turnips, some of them wooden and running to seed, my carrots wilting under attacks of carrot fly. He would observe Jean's struggling shrubs and sparsely flowering annuals. At the sight he would shut his eyes as if offended and heave a sigh. 'Bloody hell!' he would murmur to himself.

Then, as if confronted with the Holy Grail, he would suddenly become aware of the carnations, red and white, strong and beautiful. And of my bed of parsley. He would shake his head. 'Man,' he would exclaim, in awe, 'is nature no' wunnerfu'! Growin' in poverty!'

4. Wise Saws

Alec's tipple was beer. He liked his daily pint, even on a Sunday. Jean's brother Willie was landlord of the Argyll Arms and, in those days before World War II, when the licensing laws were strict, he and Alec had an understanding. As the kirk bells began to ring Alec would slip into the empty bar and be offered a hospitable refreshment.

The time came when Willie was about to be married and, as the big day approached, a new barmaid from Glasgow took over his duties in the bar. Alec heard the bells, stumped along the village street and made his way to the Inn. He was taken aback to see a blonde lady behind the counter whose voice held no friendly cadence as she inquired: 'Yes, what do you want?'

Alec swallowed. 'I'll ha'e ma pint,' he said, bravely.

'Are you a *bona fide* traveller?'

'Eh?'

'Are you a *bona fide* traveller?'

'God, naw!' said Alec, bemused. 'I'm a gairdener frae Carskiey!'

But if he knew nothing about the licensing laws Alec knew a great deal about gardening. Not about gardening in modern dress perhaps, with its emphasis on scientific and labour-saving devices of every sort; rather about gardening as a kind of folklore handed down from one generation to another.

He would wax indignant on the subject of chemical fertilizers. 'They tak' a' the guid oot o' the grun'!' he would tell us. 'Wrack an' dung, that's a' ye need. Though mind ye,' he would add, 'coo dung's the best. Weel rotted. The seaweed lasts jeest a year, but the dung bides in the grun' fur keeps.'

'If the wrack only lasts a year,' I would say, 'why use it at all?'

'Weel, the fermers ha'e aye used it. Some bloody nonsense aboot potash. Guid for potatoes an' cabbages an' that.'

'So science is creeping in after all, Alec?'

'Ach, naw! Seaweed's natural. Ye're far better tae depend on natural stuff. An' experience, of coorse. Ower muckle science an' the grun' storrs an' runs oot efter a while.'

By 'storrs' he meant 'refuses to function'. (For example, if Alec saw a horse refusing a fence in the Grand National, he would say it had 'storred'.) And he had a point. Indeed, one of the great ecological arguments of the present day concerns the same problem. Some farmers are beginning to believe that the increasing use of artificial fertilizers for inducing heavier and yet heavier crops will soon become, in the modern jargon, counterproductive.

As an unscientific amateur, I may be criticized for voicing an opinion. Nevertheless, as a citizen in what still purports to be a free and democratic country, I do so with vigour. (So much 'bureaucratization' and 'centralization' have been taking place in recent years – 1984 among them – that there may be little time left for me to exercise such freedom.) I believe that the wholesale, uneducated use of artificial aids in agriculture and horticulture, in the greedy scramble for quick profits, are leading us towards disaster, in much the same way as too much interference with nature has led to the 'dust bowls' of North America and the deforested 'deserts' of South America. (With difficulty I refrain from bringing nuclear weapons into the argument, though they constitute a parallel danger. Indeed, in this regard, a devasted, poisoned Siberian town is an example of what can happen.)

The same kind of thing is affecting medicine in the over-use of drugs. After too much dosage even penicillin becomes useless.

I know an elderly lady who once occupied a responsible secretarial post. Beset by business worries, not unconnected with a boss who preferred whisky drinking to hard work, she began to take amphetamines in order – so she thought – to boost her vitality. Then, finding she couldn't sleep at night, she resorted to sleeping pills which left her so drowsy in the morning that she had to increase her intake of amphetamines.

After months of this unnatural régime she found herself in a state of exhaustion, both physical and mental. Ideas which might have benefited the firm no longer flourished in her mind, and, bereft of intelligent management, the business crumpled and died. Only the intervention of a caring and clear-sighted doctor, who told her, brusquely, to throw all her pills into the dustbin, may have prevented her from dying, too.

I am glad to say that she now enjoys life on an old age pension augmented by her savings (appropriately taxed, of course, so that the National Health Service can put more and more business in the way of the drug manufacturers) and works happily as a housewife and on various church and social committees. Her boss? He died at a comparatively early age. The minister mourned a tragic loss, praising his 'good works' in the town as a councillor and magistrate.

The lady in question is now as comprehensively critical of the drug scene as was Alec about chemical fertilizers. But I do not agree with the argument that drugs, chemical fertilizers and pesticides should be done away with altogether. Some drugs, used by careful doctors, save lives. Some 'artificials' are good for ailing gardens. Trouble starts only when tired and overworked doctors, encouraged by drug companies intent upon adding to their wealth, thoughtlessly pander to their pain-scared, demanding patients, and when farmers and gardeners, encouraged by the manufacturers – also aiming for large profits – thoughtlessly sicken the ground with ever increasing doses of chemicals.

Nature was Alec's pillar of salt as a gardener. He had many sayings relevant to 'the ploughing and the sowing, the reaping and the mowing', especially regarding appropriate weather conditions and times of the year. He had strange tales to tell about the curative properties of various vegetables and herbs: tales which I found were also known in many other parts of the country.

I listened to them, fascinated, noting them down and writing articles about them for newspapers and magazines. (A guinea here and a guinea there made life easier for a writer intent upon establishing himself and, at the same time, making life easier for his wife and infant son.) I could not make myself believe in some of them; and now that I have had some experience of gardening – albeit in a crude and unambitious way – and, therefore, plenty of opportunities to test their practicality, I still cannot.

For example an old friend of mine used to repeat a verse which postulated that if the oak comes into leaf before the ash then gardeners will have a 'splash'. There was an addendum to this: 'If the ash before the oak, then there'll be a soak.' Talk about hedging your bets! No matter which leaf comes first it is going to rain. In any case, what is the difference between a 'splash' and a 'soak'? A 'splash' in damp Argyll may be described as a 'soak' in drouthy Kent. And what help to a gardener is that?

Alec had another one about the weather:

> If Candlemas Day (2 February) be bright and fair
> The rest o' the winter's tae come – an' mair.

For a number of years now Jean has kept a diary in which she notes (amongst other gardening and domestic information) each day's weather. According to its evidence such a prophecy is false. Neither does it support the widely held belief that a new moon on a Saturday means fine weather for a month. Oddly enough, however, Alec's dictum that if March comes in like a lion 'it gangs oot like a lamb' (and *vice versa*) seems to be nearly always true, at the Mull of Kintyre at any rate.

Like Alec and many another countryman in the Highlands and Islands of Scotland, I have found that the arrival and departure of migrant birds and the reappearance of hibernating animals can be useful in forecasting weather. The creatures themselves have no powers of prophecy and are not infallible guides – in this, I reckon, they resemble the experts on television – but they are sensitive to minute atmospheric changes. Seagulls are driven inland by the approach of a cold front. Gnats – and the swallows and house martins which prey on them – undoubtedly fly higher in fine weather and lower before rain, a habit which suggests sensitivity to moisture in the atmosphere.

'Red sky at morning is the shepherd's warning' is to some

extent true, because a redness at dawn means that the air is heavy with moisture. But a more certain intimation of rain, as Alec was forever reminding me, is a dawnlight tinged with green. (In the West of Scotland a forecast of rain is always a safe bet, no matter what the condition of the sky or the sea or of burrowing animals. And I am glad of that, toiling in my patch of porous sandy ground.)

Rural areas abound with 'weatherwise' old men. I may be counted as one of them myself, particularly in relation to gardening and golf. My forecasting of weather is generally based on the charts which appear on television, but I seldom admit this, preferring to look sagely at the sea and sky, to sniff the wind whining in over the hills at the Mull and then to utter some hopeful or hopeless saying on the lines of 'Rain before seven, dry before eleven' (if there is golf in prospect) or 'Between the hours of twelve and two, we'll see what the day will do' (if I am being pressed into digging the garden too soon after breakfast).

Some day somebody is going to quote at me yet another saying: 'Folk that are weatherwise are seldom otherwise.'

Alec had also a liberal store of 'knowledge' concerning when and how to sow and plant.

His plentiful advice on potatoes and potato planting had a mystic ring to it which appealed to the Celtic element in my nature but not to a vein of scepticism which I probably inherited from Scandinavian ancestors.

He kept telling me that as a Scot I ought never to buy seed from England: seed potatoes should always come from *north* of where they are planted. (I put it to him once that potato planters in Greenland might be somewhat sceptical about this. His only answer was a sigh and the kind of sad yet loving look which Christians reserve for unbelievers.) They should also be put in the ground on a rising tide, he said, so that they may grow with it.

There is a Hebridean saying that the best time to be born is on a rising tide; and it is reported by Adomnan that St Columba was born under such circumstances. I wonder if the 'rising tide' belief in respect of potato planting had its origin in this legend?

Incidentally, the same Columba had a 'bounteous' garden in Iona. No wonder: he had plenty of gardeners to tend it, in the persons of numerous disciples and monks. Lucky man! And the soil there is wonderfully fertile, requiring no chemical additives to 'improve' its products.

At 'the port of the coracle' (where, it is said, Columba and his disciples landed in their little boat) gannets dive offshore and oyster-catchers wade at the edge of the white sands, just as they must have done more than fourteen centuries ago.

Indeed, behind the dunes, larks and peewits keep watch upon the Cathedral and the Druid stones. And upon the king-cups and the bog myrtle and the yellow St John's wort, a sprig of which the Saint always carried inside his robe (because of his admiration for John the Baptist) and which in the Gaelic is called 'the armpit package of Columba'.

Sea scent and flower scent mingle in an air of crystal clarity. At least, such has always been my experience. But it occurs to me that because the island is so flat and exposed gardeners in Iona (including the saintly ones) must often have uttered less than saintly words about the gales which often blow across it.

St Columba, of course, did not grow potatoes and would know nothing of blackened and bedraggled shaws. Nobody in the British Isles knew that potatoes even existed until Sir John Hawkins brought some from South America to Ireland in 1565 and Sir Francis Drake introduced them to England in 1585. And it was many years later that potatoes grown in Ireland came to be planted in Virginia in North America, an odd circumstance in the history of a vegetable which was cultivated and eaten by the Peruvians at least as early as 750 BC.

Shakespeare's knowledge of gardens – and particularly herbal gardens – seems to have been extensive. In *Hamlet* he wrote: 'There is no ancient gentlemen but gardeners, ditchers and grave-makers; they hold up Adam's profession.' And, in the same play, he gives practical advice:

> 'tis an unweeded garden,
> That grows to seed; things rank and gross in nature
> Possess it merely.

At one time it was believed that the potato had an aphrodisiac quality, a quaint notion which did not escape the attention of the Bard. When Falstaff wanted vigour to tackle the Merry Wives he cried, in a kind of ecstasy: 'Let the sky rain potatoes!'

Alec must also have had a folk memory concerning this belief. Skirting round the subject with a knowing leer appropriate in the company of the minister's eldest son, he once said to me, in a hoarse whisper: 'Gin ye want tae be Cock o' the North, son, eat plenty o' tatties!'

But Alec was right in much of what he said about planting and sowing. He was a keen bird fancier as well as a gardener, often trapping 'wee linties' (finches) under riddles baited with oats and keeping them as house companions for a time before releasing them again. 'Plant yer tatties,' he used to say, 'when Wee Willie Wagtail comes in the spring.' That, I have found, is good advice, because Wee Willie Wagtail, sensible bird, does not appear in my garden until the weather has become mild and the ground has lost its winter chill.

A friend of mine who went to farm in Essex was greatly amused to find a saying among the rustics there: 'The earth is ready for planting and sowing when you can sit on it with your trousers down and it feels all right.' I think they must have been pulling his leg. Strangely enough, however, Alec had a couplet along the same lines, which he used to quote with 'laughter loud and shrill'. (My publisher has censored this one, but it played – very coarsely – upon the words 'earth' and 'erse'.)

The only advice which, from my own experience, I can offer about potatoes is that they should never be planted until their shoots have grown strong in their boxes and the ground has become dry and reasonably warm.

There seems to be no point in hurrying to get them in, especially in Scotland. I have planted early varieties in February, March and April and, in the outcome, they have all been ready for digging at approximately the same time: that is, in the first week of July. As for late potatoes, the finest crop of Golden Wonders I ever had was planted on 23 April, Jock's tenth birthday. I remember this, because while I was dourly digging the drills, and scattering compost along them, and rubbing superfluous shoots off the dark, dry seed, he and his party pals were stampeding back and forth across the ground in violent games of cops and robbers.

I suggest that for potatoes dung or seaweed should be used as fertilizer. In North Uist and in the garden at the manse Midlothian Earlies were always grown in seaweed and, though smallish in size, they had a flavour which young people today, buying anonymous potatoes in anonymous plastic bags, have never known. So good, indeed, were the Padre's potatoes that on one occasion my brother John, at the ravenous age of eighteen, ate twenty-seven of them at a sitting. He suffered no harm; but now I scarcely think that as a distinguished gynaecologist he would recommend such indulgence even to his pregnant patients.

I used to grow Sharpe's Express in this natural way, and Jean and I looked forward to eating them in July like gourmets panting after caviar. Unfortunately, Common Market regulations have now done a 'thumbs down' on Sharpe's Express. (Some nonsense about it not being sufficiently disease resistant.) I grow Wilja instead, a new variety which is almost but not quite as tasty. I may say, unofficially and in confidence, that in Scotland there exists a black market in Sharpe's Express. Many of us, glad to cock a snook at the EEC, still enjoy a meal of them. If you fancy a pound or two of seed . . .

'Artificials' do ensure a crop of large tubers but they generally do so at the expense of taste. 'Go for bulk' seems to be the motto of most modern food producers. But going for bulk simply means going for higher profits, and clever packaging and marketing conceals from the consumer the fact that he is missing out on a much superior – and much healthier – 'natural' taste.

An English gardener, who was also a poet, once declared that artificial fertilizers make the soil 'deaf to the music of the spheres'. I understand what he meant. In another context I wish some politicians, dependent for their success upon advertising agencies, might understand it, too.

*   *   *

When he farmed Brunerican, I used to get manure from Jean's nephew, Donnie McKerral: rich cow dung held together by the byre bedding straw brushed out with it each morning. Now that Donnie has become a haulage contractor I get my annual supply from another neighbour, Richard Semple, owner of Low Cattadale farm behind the hill. He brings it to me in a tractor and trailer and, when the stuff has been unloaded – sometimes in a heap adjacent to the back door which may cause some domestic acrimony because of Jean's fastidious nose – there is an opportunity to discuss matters of kirk and state over a warming dram of whisky. We have no planes or trains to catch; and even as we exchange views productivity continues in the soil outside.

To farmers as well as to gardeners dung is a precious commodity. It is spread on fields before they are ploughed and also on grass to encourage its growth for silage. Without it the farmers' fertilizer bills would be even more enormous than they are. In this material age, therefore, when the whole ethos of society appears to be money-grubbing, it may be remarkable to some that I get my dung for nothing. But in a country environment, where values are seldom represented in material terms, it is not so remarkable.

Caring for neighbours and living with them in amicable understanding seems to be an idea which, in a national sense, has become trampled down in a ruthless struggle for monetary advantage. I believe this struggle to be of urban origin, refuelled in recent years by the micro-chip revolution. In rural areas like Southend at the Mull of Kintyre we are nearer the earth and, therefore, less likely to become insensitive to the claims of ordinary humanity. Computers cannot measure a gardener's desire to share with others the plant life he has helped to create or a farmer's instinctive knowledge of how best to treat his neighbours, his cattle and the good earth.

So I get my dung from Richard, free. In due time I share some of my early vegetables with his wife, Elizabeth, who entertains summer visitors in her hospitable house. No money changes hands. The idea of monetary profit does not come into it. But the idea of profit in terms of friendship and good will certainly does.

I get my seaweed for nothing as well.

After a storm from the south which causes huge grey waves, tossing white manes of spray, to gallop in and thunder up the shore below Achnamara, the wrack is piled on the sand. (Our windows are also encrusted with salt, which is less than pleasing to Jean, who dislikes obscurity of any kind.) I put on my wellingtons, find an old sack among the lumber in the garage, put a tattered rubber glove on my right hand and scramble down over the rocks to scoop it up and win a harvest.

In the absence of storms there is always seaweed to be found in the Stinking Hole.

I believe that the best kind of weed for the garden is the bladder variety. Long-fronded driftweed is also good. For a sandy garden like mine, however, the bulky, long-stemmed 'tangle' is of lesser value because it takes so long to disintegrate in the ground. The 'tangle o' the isles' has a ring to it in the song; but it does not sing a particularly cheery horticultural tune. It is also heavy to carry for a geriatric who likes to conserve most of his physical energy for the golf.

5. And Modern Instances

From Alec – as well as from my mother in days gone by – I received much advice on the use of 'natural' pesticides. (The Padre never bothered about such details. It may be that he depended on the power of prayer.)

When I started to garden at first, before World War II, my main enemy was the carrot fly. Sandy ground, I had been told, is good for carrots. I sowed plenty, therefore, in those early years; but almost always they grew fresh for a time and then slowly died as the fly chewed and burrowed into their flesh. My mother's suggestion was that I should spread dried southernwood along the drills, so that the flies might be attracted to it rather than to the carrots. Alec's was that I ought to sow parsley or spring onions among them to disguise the smell. I have to report that though I carried out both suggestions (there was plenty of southernwood in the manse garden) my carrot flies paid no attention to the parsley or onion smells, and the southernwood – if they ate it at all – did not spoil their appetite for carrots.

Something that has always intrigued me is that farmers can grow carrots in their fields without risk of their being attacked by fly. The answer, according to Richard – and according to other farming neighbours like Jim McPhee and Archie Cameron, who are always willing to supply me with expert knowledge during a round of golf, especially if they are winning at the time and inclined to feel superior – lies in the fact that fields are cultivated on a system of rotation which allows them to lie fallow for relatively long periods.

Field carrots may be grown in the same place only once every seven years or so. This means that fly families do not become established in that particular piece of ground, because in seven years, without carrots, they would starve to death. They are inclined, therefore, to proliferate in snug little gardens, where carrots are always available within a yard or two, even though the gardener does change their position from year to year. (Rotation of crops, horticulturally speaking, is a different practice from rotation of crops, agriculturally speaking. I hope to deal with this subject later on, if my nerve holds out.)

The onion fly was another enemy which seemed to ignore the only natural repellent which Alec and my mother could suggest. This was to grow parsley close to the onion bed. Even surrounded by a miniature hedge of parsley my onions still wilted and, usually in the late summer, little white bugs burrowed into the bulbs and sucked them to death.

For some years, in my new garden, I was able to grow cabbages of a reasonable size. Then, receiving news on their private communications system of a kindly new gardener in a field above the shore – a gardener, moreover, who appeared to be something of a mug as far as his defences were concerned – the white butterflies began to arrive. Jean adored them for their grace and apparent friendliness. I have seen her standing, entranced, talking to one which balanced delicately on the palm of her hand. It was only when scores of caterpillars suddenly began to infest the cabbage leaves and chew them into tattered skeletons that I understood the real purpose of their visit.

Alec saw the caterpillars and shook his head, in much the same lugubrious fashion as he might have contemplated a line of advancing Germans in World War I. 'Spray them wi' sea watter,' was his advice. 'Maybe this year it's too late. But next year gi'e them the treatment early, afore they mak' sic a mess.'

Next year, as fate befell, I was absent from home serving my country in foreign fields, and the condition of the vegetables in Achnamara garden was far from my thoughts. Many years later, however, I remembered what Alec had said and experimented with his 'cure'. It works. I can testify that it works. Salt water sprayed on cabbage plants definitely helps to keep caterpillars at bay.

But then, in those prewar years, there developed an even

more serious threat. This was the club root fly, which caused my young cabbages to wither and die soon after they had been transplanted in June.

Alec had little comfort to offer. 'It's like the bloody measles. Either ye get it or ye dinna. But I've heard it said if ye put in plenty o' dung the cabbage roots will grow sae big an' strong that the wee buggers can eat their fill withoot damagin' the plant.' So I shovelled in dung. But still my cabbages died.

Strangely enough, my enemies did not – and still do not – include slugs. One reason may be the salty atmosphere in which we live, because slugs, I understand, are allergic to too much salt. Another may be the fact that my soil is so basically poor that they have never considered it worth their while to trek in our direction from lusher inland pastures. In a way I am disappointed about this, because I should love to try out the 'natural cure' recommended by a gardener on television. Sink a bowl of beer in the ground, he told us. The slugs will be attracted to it, and as they squirm over the side they will slip in and drown. 'Replace the beer once a week,' suggested the expert, in a practical postscript.

But even without the help of slugs my foes were able, at the beginning, to win victories all along the line. I felt dispirited, inclined to give up the idea of growing vegetables and allow the garden to become a habitat for sprawling veronicas, rhododendrons and fuchsias, which, like Jean's carnations, had become well established. And, indeed, not until World War II had become but a memory did I shoulder off despair and decide upon a planned counterattack.

> Again to the battle, Achaians!
> Our hearts bid the tyrants defiance;
> Our land, the first garden of Liberty's tree –
> It has been, and shall yet be, the land of the free!

And now, as it happens, after much travail and error – and after much soul-searching as an exponent of 'natural' gardening – I seem to have routed large numbers of the enemy. For many years now my carrots (mainly Autumn King) have grown large and healthy and juicy, enabling us to store them in

sand in the autumn and continue eating them until the following April or May. This is fortunate for Jean, because carrots
are her favourite vegetable. And her opinion of her husband
as a gardener has risen on account of it.

But I have to confess that my success (if an amateur may be
allowed the use of the word, even in a relative sense) appears to
be due almost entirely to artificial pesticides. Southernwood
and spring onions failed. Bromophos and Gamma BHC are
the weapons I used to put the barbarians to flight.

My onion crop, too, has now become a source of pride. And
this is fortunate for me, because they are *my* favourite vegetable. (In the *Canterbury Tales* Geoffrey Chaucer had a word
for me:

> Wel loved he garleek, oynon, and eek leeks,
> And for to drinken strong wyn, reed as blood.

Though I might add that I enjoy a glass of amber whisky
equally as well as one of claret.)

Growing my onions from sets planted usually about the
middle of March, I loosen them from the ground in late
August and let them bask in what sunshine there is until the
first week in September. Then I gather them in and store them
in our dry and airy loft, laying them separately on an old
length of Netlon windbreak slung between two of the rafters.
If Jean rations them carefully against my constant demands
they last until the following April.

But though I always grow some parsley near them, I have to
admit that credit for the rout of the onion fly must go to the
calomel paste in which I dip the sets before planting and to a
light dusting of Gamma BHC which I give the growing plants
in mid-May and late June.

I seem also to have freed my cabbages of white butterflies
and their voracious young (in the shape of caterpillars). Sometimes I do spray them with sea water, as Alec advised, but I
also dust them with Derris, just to make sure. And – perhaps
the best safeguard of all – I keep an eye on my plants and pick
off any unwelcome guests if and when they appear.

There may be something in Alec's theory that plenty of

dung encourages so much growth in the cabbage stem that the root fly can eat its fill without damaging the head. But since I started to dip the roots of the young transplants in calomel paste there has been no sign of 'the wee buggers' in my garden.

'Natural cures' are all very well; but, since Alec's day – and my mother's day – it should be remembered that scientific inoculation against measles has rendered the disease almost nonexistent. And if doctors use 'artificial aids', why shouldn't gardeners?

At the back of my mind, however, there lurks a feeling almost of guilt. What about 'the music of the spheres'?

The 'gremlins' I find most difficult to deal with are birds, young rabbits and moles.

Sparrows attack young green plants with a ferocity in startling contrast to their usually friendly attitude. Blackbirds and thrushes can do damage, too.

Young rabbits squeeze through tiny holes in gates and netting and can devour a whole row of infant lettuce in a single night. They are like Attila and his Huns, spreading devastation wherever they go. Somebody once told me that they dislike carrot leaves. More than once, during morning inspection, I have found several drills of early carrots completely destroyed by them.

As for moles, they, too, in a single night, can heave and hump their way through a nursery bed, killing off a huge range of young growth ready for transplanting. Jules Verne's burrowing machine caused a terrible upheaval as it approached the surface; and what it could do, so can moles. A trim and tidy lawn can resemble a battlefield after a dawn attack by those small, cuddlesome monsters. Do you realize that if human beings were as strong and capable as moles, a gang of us could dig out the Channel Tunnel with our bare hands in about a week?

What should a gardener do about the birds, the rabbits, the moles?

There is, of course, a simple answer: one which might be recommended by a Hitler or a Stalin. Eliminate them. Kill them off.

The trouble is, all faithful gardeners are fond of the little horrors. In moments of stress the idea of cold and callous slaughter often arises; but it is seldom if ever put into action. (Which indicates, I suppose, what awful hypocrites we are. We use pesticides to do away with carrot fly, onion fly and club root fly and feel no guilt. Yet carrot fly, onion fly and club root fly are living creatures just the same. Is there a philosopher who can bring me any comfort in respect of this problem?) Then, if the gardener has a wife like mine, to whom blackbirds, thrushes and sparrows come flocking as she calls them to breakfast, the situation becomes even more difficult. Even fraught.

For example, there is George the Third. He is a stout and glossy blackbird who spends the winter eating happily out of Jean's hand. In the spring he brings his drab little wife to share the feast; and when his family appears in summer he brings them, too – large, clumsy chicks who gobble up food like a gang of weightlifters. In late summer he comes alone again; and perhaps because he feels relieved at having shed the responsibility of a wife and family, he sits on the Hydro Board pole behind Achnamara and sings to us, morning and evening.

And what marvellous songs he sings. They all begin with the same seven notes – the first seven notes of 'If I Were a Blackbird'. (You may be too young to remember the song. In its day, as sung and whistled by Ronnie Ronalde, it topped the charts.)

It was George the Third's grandfather – the original George – who first made Achnamara his favourite family hotel. No doubt, in a year or two, one of the gangling chicks now being brought to Jean's attention will develop into George the Forth.

Then there is Dugald, who is a robin. He spends his winter in the Achnamara hotel and, during summer, departs for other less crowded resorts. I expect he has a girlfriend somewhere. Or maybe more than one, judging by his confident, even brash behaviour.

Dugald likes it when I make a start with the digging in October or November. He operates immediately behind me. Scrambling and sliding excitedly up and down the slope formed as I turn the earth, he pecks out the suddenly exposed grubs and worms. If I stop to rest on my spade at the end of a drill he stands there, head on one side, regarding me with a kind of reproach. 'Get on with it, man! I'm hungry, if you're not!' I tell him he's a greedy, ill-bred little so-and-so and make threatening gestures with my spade. He remains standing, less than a yard away, unmoved.

So what is a gardener to do about the Georges and the Dugalds in his world?

Mine live like lords off Jean's hospitality; and yet, ungratefully, if they feel so inclined – or, perhaps, if they require an aperient after the rich food they consume at the back door – they will attack my young lettuces and cabbages. And, of course, my strawberries. Evil churns in my mind. But the example of Cain usually comes to haunt me, and murderous thoughts quickly evaporate. With a sigh I settle to the laborious task of arranging threads above my young lettuces and nets above the cabbages and strawberries.

But then it may happen that George becomes entangled in the strawberry net – his beak stained red after a dawnlight debauch – and Jean has to disentangle him with such loving care that more gaps are torn in the net and I have to repair it, muttering. Meanwhile George, unconcerned, is singing a happy song atop his pole.

In moments of annoyance, when my lettuces lie in tatters and carrot-tops are snipped off by sharp beaks, I recall wryly, on the verge of wishful thinking, a story which is a favourite in our local Drama Club.

It concerns a young lady teacher in Glasgow who was not a fan of Robert Burns. She liked poetry of what she called 'a more refined nature'.

One day she said to her pupils: 'Now, boys and girls, please listen to these four lines of poetry:

> In winter, when the days are cold,
>   The birds fly off to Spain.
> In summer, when the days are warm,
>   They fly back home again.

Now, I want you to go home and add four lines of poetry to

my four lines, and tomorrow we'll see how much you have learnt about the art of writing poetry.'

Wee Jimmy went home. 'Hey, maw, the teacher wants us tae add fower lines o' poetry tae her fower lines, an' I canna write poetry. Whit'll I dae?'

'Never you mind, son. Yar faither's at a Burns Supper the nicht, but when he comes hame I'll get him to write something for ye. He thinks he's a great poet, especially efter a Burns Supper!'

Next day the teacher smiled at her class. 'Now, boys and girls, you remember my four lines of poetry:

> In winter, when the days are cold,
>   The birds fly off to Spain.
> In summer, when the days are warm,
>   They fly back home again.

A wee hand went up.

'Yes, Jimmy,' she said. 'Let's hear your four lines.'

> The – birds were – flying – hame – frae Spain.
>   They met a – bloody hawk,
> Who pookit a' – their feathers – *oot*
>   An' made the buggers walk.

*   *   *

Gardeners who own a cat are fortunate. Jean once owned a cat whose name was Ian. He was so well fed that the notion of killing and eating birds never occurred to him. But his hunting and sporting instincts remained strong. He obviously enjoyed keeping an eye on the garden and, with dramatic leaps and bounds, chasing marauders away. He himself, however, was something of a nuisance, thinking nothing at times of excavating earthen 'loos' among my turnips. (Why the turnip ground should have constituted his favourite bathroom I can offer no explanation.)

Ian, of course, believed he was human.

His mother was an aristocrat, the Lady Susan, his father a disreputable tramp known to everyone in the parish as Old Donald. This probably accounted for contrasting elements in his character and appearance. His fastidious cleanliness, for example, compared with intermittent bouts of swashbuckling violence. His underside so white and smooth compared with a main covering of shaggy grey.

One afternoon I sat typing at my desk, with the Lady Susan curled up in an armchair by the fire. We were alone in the house, Jean being at a Woman's Guild meeting and Jock at school. Suddenly, to my horror, I realized that the Lady Susan was beginning to have kittens. I picked her up, along with the first of her brood, and carried her out by the back door. Ian was born on the way to the garage, falling softly on the gravel at my feet.

For me it was a traumatic experience, and when Jean and Jock returned in the evening they were reminded forcibly that the Lady Susan was *their* cat and that it ought to have been their job, not mine, to attend her in a gynaecological crisis.

From that day Ian purred with a happy vigour which saved him from the usual fate of unwanted kittens. Having been 'dressed' at an early age, he went on to enjoy a gentleman's life, the life to which his mother's aristocratic lineage so well fitted him.

During the day he rested by the fire, while I laboured with words to earn his keep. In a bygone age Beverley Nichols would have called me non-F, meaning that I was not besotted about felines; but Ian and I lived together amicably enough. From me he expected none of the affection lavished on him by Jean and Jock. If he wished to leave the room, however, he was always willing to let me know, aware that he could depend upon my co-operation in a slow and dignified exit. But seldom did he respond to my parting exhortation: 'And don't go near my turnips!'

At one time Jean kept her cats shut in at night. Later she discovered that full feline health depends on their being free to move about in the nocturnal air. After dark, therefore, Ian was put in the garage, where he had a luxurious bed. But the door was left partially open, and he spent a lot of time in the surrounding fields. (That leaving the garage door open allowed sea-spray to drift in and cause rusty stains on the car and the lawn mower was unimportant to Jean and Jock compared with Ian's wellbeing.)

There was no need for Ian to hunt. He was well fed on fish, red meat and milk with the chill taken off. (It sounds ridiculous, but I can assure you that he would turn his nose up at milk taken directly from the 'frig'.) But as I enjoyed my golf, so he enjoyed his chosen sport, and we often found the results on the doorstep – no birds from the garden, but mice, rabbits, even an occasional weasel from the fields.

Few cats will face up to a weasel, a cunning and ferocious fighter. The tougher the opponent, however, the better Ian liked it. After a successful night he used to stalk into my workroom with an air of aloof but unmistakable satisfaction, in much the same way as my golfing friend, Sandy Watson, comes into the clubhouse after a good round in the monthly medal.

Before he learned road-sense Ian was struck by a car outside Achnamara front gate. His head was gashed and we despaired of his life. But after a few days he was tempted to swallow a morsel of fish, and from that moment he began to recover, though the sight of one eye had gone.

The accident seemed to make no difference to his skill as a hunter. On the other hand, as a brave invalid, he played even more cunningly than before on Jean's and Jock's sympathy. Now, instead of on the hearth rug, he passed most evenings in the lap of his choice, purring. Once he made an attempt to occupy my armchair, no doubt with a view to making it his own. But in this case I stood up courageously for my rights, even though my nearest and dearest did not offer even token support.

Ian grew old along with us. As he approached the age of twenty, he became deaf – probably a delayed result of his accident – and decayed teeth made eating difficult. We were coming to the sad conclusion that he would have to be put down when the situation was unexpectedly resolved. One morning our local doctor – who was a friend of his – found his dead body on the road, about a hundred yards from the house. He had been run over by a lorry which, as we guessed, he had failed to hear.

By then Jock was working in Glasgow, and Jean refused to go near the mangled remains. So, as at his birth, I officiated at his death. I buried him deep on the shore, the place of many a happy hunting.

Besides threads, nets and cats, the gardener's only other 'natural' defence against birds is a scarecrow, preferably one with a wind-propelled whirligig attached.

I have erected many scarecrows, some merely wooden posts with a child's toy 'whirlie' on top, others elaborately dressed in old clothes discarded by the Drama Club. For me, none of them has ever worked. Following the example of George and Dugald, who are not daft, sparrows, finches, even crows and seagulls soon begin to use them as comfortable platforms from which to survey the garden and decide upon the kind of vegetable they fancy for their next meal. But a gardener whose spouse is less protective of the feathered 'darlings' than mine is may – I repeat may – find scarecrows to be effective.

Then the rabbits.

No matter with how much netting I surround the garden, young rabbits always seem able to find a way in. How to deal with them? Here again a cat may be useful – a cat, of course, with a proper killer instinct. Ian's idea of scaring rabbits was to join them in wild games of hide-and-seek among my cabbage plants. And cabbage plants do not appreciate bounding bundles of fur crashing into them and breaking their stems.

To generalize about cats, however, is as futile as to generalize about people.

We had another cat once, whose name was Trooshlach, a word from the Gaelic meaning 'rubbish'. He was a big, black, 'doctored' tom, lazy, good-natured, friendly to a fault, especially when cream or fish appeared on the table. But as far as brains were concerned, his name was appropriate. So useless was he as a hunter that the house became infested with mice – giant, overfed fieldmice which infiltrated our defences from the cultivated terrain behind us.

One afternoon I was working at my desk when a scuttling noise occurred. Carefully a mouse emerged from behind the bookcase. I leapt to my feet with murderous intent. The mouse scuttled back, as agilely as Jerry in the cartoon.

Trooshlach was resting by the fire.

'All right,' I said, carrying him across to the bookcase and planting him down at the point where the mouse had appeared. 'You sit here and wait. When Jerry comes out again, nab him!'

Yawning slightly, but with apparent good grace, Trooshlach settled down to obey my instructions.

Time passed. I was worrying at a phrase which refused to sing for me when another small sound disturbed my concentration. I looked up. The mouse had appeared, only inches away from my bold, black sentry.

As I watched, Trooshlach raised a paw, no doubt impelled to do so by some long submerged hunter instinct. The paw wavered above the mouse, as if ready to strike.

Then, to my amazement, the mouse moved on – directly under the paw – generating speed as it did so. Its tail disappeared round the partially open door. Trooshlach remained in a statuesque pose, paw still held high, gazing stupidly at the spot where the mouse no longer was.

'You great idiot!' I said to him.

He turned his head and lowered his paw. His expression was one of puzzlement. He seemed to be saying: 'What exactly did you want me to do?'

I knew exactly what I wanted to do – with him and with the mouse. But the adrenalin produced by annoyance had suddenly caused the phrase I was struggling with to make music. I got back to work. Trooshlach returned to the fire. He stretched and yawned again as if shrugging metaphorical shoulders.

I suffer from another handicap in my continuing campaign against young rabbits.

Some years ago, soon after Ian's death, a young rabbit took up residence under a disorganized clump of heath and veronica immediately adjacent to the vegetable garden. In the night watches, while I slept, it began to nibble at my lettuces, cabbages and carrots. At last, driven to exasperation, I planned violent retribution.

But how to coax this creature out of its tangled lair, so that I might aim a lethal swipe at it? No matter how madly I beat upon the bushes it always refused to come out. Sometimes I would glimpse it far down among the twigs and leaves and make a quick thrust; but long before my graip could reach the target area it had moved slinkily and silently to a safer spot.

Jean became schizophrenic. On the one hand she sympathized with me for having worked so hard in the garden only to find my rewards being snatched away by a pirate. On the other hand she was terrified that in my rage I might kill the rabbit, which, in soft language which accorded ill with my mood, she described as 'a wee pet'. When I made my attacks on the bushes she was always there, torn with anxiety concerning the outcome.

One morning I banged about with my graip and, perhaps drowsy and unprepared after a night's gluttony, the rabbit emerged. Only half grown, it looked clean and fresh and smug. I made a wild lunge in its direction but tripped on a root of veronica and fell among the cabbages. The rabbit loped away with contemptuous ease and took cover behind a long concrete edging tile which lay against the wall of the garage.

But that was its error. I had it now. Brushing myself down, I approached the garage and held the graip high. 'Ease that tile away from the wall,' I instructed Jean.

'No, no, please! Don't kill him!'

'Don't kill him! That rabbit is a menace! Starving us to death!'

'Poor wee thing! He's lying there, terrified!'

'I should hope so! Ease away the tile!'

'No, no, please! You realize what you're doing, don't you? You're playing God.'

'What?'

'You're always writing about St Columba. Remember that story you often tell about when he was a little boy and he bent down to take a trout from the river and the poet Gemman said to him, "How would *you* like it if God stretched down His hand and tried to kill *you*?"'

'The trout wasn't eating God's lettuces.'

'That's completely illogical. And blasphemous besides.'

'Give me strength!' I said.

'The poor wee rabbit hasn't much strength.'

'What has that got to do with it?'

'Everything,' she said.

I lowered the graip. 'Well, if I spare its blasted life it's not going to spend the remainder of it in our garden!'

'Of course not. Wait a minute.'

She put a hand under the tile and presently withdrew it, holding the rabbit. Having fondled it, uttering low-pitched words of endearment, she said to me: 'Now, take out the car. Drive me down to the graveyard and I'll pop him over the wall. He'll find the best grass in the parish there.'

It was the first time I had played chauffeur to a rabbit, and I prayed that on our journey nobody would see us. Thankfully nobody did. The pirate was left to enjoy luxury among the tombstones, a fate better than he deserved; and for the rest of the season the garden flourished.

Except for a flank attack by white maggots on some of my onion crop. I had omitted to coat a number of the sets in calomel paste.

6. Moles at the Mull

There is an ancient Gaelic saying to the effect that 'when moles reach the Mull loud and lusty men will follow, and beetles will bring woe to Kintyre'.

The fact is, moles have been burrowing close to the Mull for centuries, most of them, I reckon – at one time or another – through the ground which is now my garden.

No doubt our Celtic ancestors, cowering in their dark little houses of stone and thatch, whispered the saying to one another when the Norsemen came in the eighth century and made the island of Sanda, two miles away across the water from my front door, a safe 'haven' for their long ships. (Sanda is a modern name. Up until last century it was called Avon.)

No doubt they repeated it when Robert the Bruce took refuge from his rampaging enemies in the Castle of Dunaverty, the ruins of which are picked out by the sun as I look across the bay. And no doubt, in 1647, the MacDonald garrison of that same castle spoke about it, too, during the siege which ended in their massacre by Leslie's republican army, aided and abetted by the Marquis of Argyll, *Gillesbuig Gruamach*, chief of Clan Campbell.

We ourselves certainly remembered it when Paul McCartney purchased his little farm outside Campbeltown, though an acquaintance of mine, famed for his 'wit', chose to quote only part of it. 'I'll tell ye, the prophecy has come true,' he told me, deadpan. 'When the moles reach the Mull the beetles will follow. God help my potatoes!'

And now that oil is being sought in the Firth of Clyde near Sanda and oil rigs at the bottom of my garden have become a possibility, we are remembering it again.

But the Norsemen, having given names to many of the

farms in Kintyre and a blond colouring to many of the local population, went away at last. Robert the Bruce escaped to the island of Rathlin, across the North Channel, where he had his notable confrontation with a spider. In 1955, to pay his debts, the Duke of Argyll – descendant of the Marquis who 'waded in blood' at Dunaverty in 1647 – sold off almost all his land in Kintyre; and so the Campbells have departed, too.

Paul McCartney, far from injuring the potato crop, composed his famous song, 'Mull of Kintyre', which has enabled newsmen to describe all murders, shipwrecks and aircraft accidents within fifty miles of it on land, sea or in the air as having taken place 'near the Mull of Kintyre'. And now, though the farm of High Park still belongs to him, we see little of Paul. He seems to have departed, too.

Today we have worries about an invasion of 'loud and lusty' men intent upon building oil storage tanks in the bird sanctuary on Sanda and among the sand dunes of the golf course. We also suspect that the sea wrack we carry up from the shore for our fields and gardens may soon become coated with oil and, therefore, useless as fertilizer. And we are afraid that the rivers and the sea may become so polluted that we can no longer eat the fish taken out of them.

But we know that if and when the oil rigs come, bringing material benefits to many, they will not stay here for ever – black Salvador Dali skeletons upon a MacTaggart seascape – and that eventually the Mull of Kintyre will resume its douce, though intermittently exciting march through history.

We also know that, unlike human adventurers and man-made machines, the moles will always be with us. Not necessarily in my garden, but in the region of the Mull.

At the beginning – and, indeed, up until the past few years – they have often threatened to turn Achnamara into a disaster area. They burrowed in from the field behind us, searching for the worms and grubs which are their usual diet and, at the same time, constructing tunnels leading to their water supply, a spring which bubbles up on the shore near Achnamara front gate. Marking the lines of their advance, piles of earth would suddenly appear amongst my vegetables and on the lawn. (Old Donald MacLean, who, fifty years ago, used to be hired by the farmers to catch rabbits and moles, once told me that a single 'moudiewart' – the Scots word for mole – can travel through a quarter of an acre of ground in a couple of hours.)

Against Jean's wishes I first experimented with a trap supplied by a neighbouring farmer. This was made of wood, a hollow cylinder in the shape of an average tunnel with a slit in one side through which was inserted a loop of thin wire attached to a spring. The loop was secured to the bottom of the cylinder by means of a trip mechanism. Then I covered it up again, leaving the top end of the spring above the surface so that I could see if and when it was activated.

In several years of endeavour I caught two moles. I buried their bodies on the shore and said nothing to Jean and Jock about them. But this made no difference at all to the number of heaps which intermittently disfigured the premises; and, in the end, I came to the conclusion that traps were ineffective.

I remembered how old Donald had often told me in confidence that he had no faith in traps either. 'Ye'd need a hunner traps in a field tae mak' ony difference. I use them jeest tae keep the fermers happy. An' tae win a few skins for masel'.' But at one time, more than half a century ago, rag-and-bone merchants paid good money for moleskins. They were used in the fur trade and in the manufacture of 'moleskin breeks'. It was his trousers which provided Patrick McGill's 'Moleskin Joe' with his nickname.

I thought once of using strychnine, which is sometimes the farmer's answer to the problem. (It is injected into worms which are then let loose in the tunnels.) But I disliked the idea of my vegetables being grown in ground containing a deadly poison; and Jean, of course, would have made my life a misery had I even mentioned strychnine. In any case, I was aware that the farmer who owned the field behind us had used both traps and strychnine and that, despite all his efforts, the molehills in his ground had become more numerous than ever. I put the thought from my mind.

From time to time I asked knowledgeable gardeners for their advice: elderly people not yet completely involved in the modern horticultural revolution who might have heard of some old-fashioned 'natural' defences against moles.

Willie the Bomber laughed in his beard. He was a contemporary of Old Alec's and had earned his unlikely sobriquet in World War I by reason of his reputation as a violent thrower of grenades.

'So yer gairden's fu' o' moles?' he said. 'Did ye ever hear the auld word – moles in yer gairden mean that ye're in debt!'

'A great help that is!' I said, thinking guiltily of my overdraft.

'I dinna ha'e moles masel',' he went on smugly. 'But I've heard it said it's no' a bad thing tae put sprigs o' whins or holly or maybe broken gless doon their holes.'

So I tried the sharp-edged treatment. Showing not the slightest sign of inconvenience, the moles went on using Achnamara front lawn as a staging post. Presumably, if they found their way blocked by prickly leaves or slivers of glass they simply tunnelled round the obstruction. No doubt in a matter of minutes.

Wee Annie Mary was an exponent of organic gardening long before the idea became 'fashionable'. She suggested a 'cure' handed down by her grandmother, who, it was said, had the second sight. This was to find the largest molehill, dig into it until the tunnel was exposed and then put in a cut bulb of garlic or onion.

I tried that. The moles continued to plague us.

One morning, at breakfast, Jean said: 'The moles have started again along the edge of the avenue. You'll just have to do something about them.'

'Good Gordon Highlanders, I've been trying to do something about them for as long as I can remember! What about doing something yourself?'

'Well, you're the gardener. Or so you tell everybody.'

Suddenly my porridge had lost its savour. 'That's a calumny! I give you full credit for the flowers and the shrubs. Not that they're much better than . . .'

'What has that got to do with moles?'

Has any other husband the same difficulty in arguing with his wife? Patiently I said: 'Nothing. Nothing at all. We were talking about moles. All right, I'll have another go with the trap.'

'I,' she said, 'have a better idea.'

'To get rid of the moles?'

'Yes.'

'Then for heaven's sake tell me!'

'Annie Mary's granny said that an onion smell might scare them away.'

'I tried that. No earthly good.'

'I know. But a woman with the second sight may have known that moles react to bad smells.'

'As far as I'm concerned an onion has a beautiful smell.'

'But you're not a mole.'

'So what?'

'I'm going to try paraffin,' she said. 'You clear up the breakfast dishes. I'll go and do it.'

She is like tnat. No sensible discussion. No planning. Action this day. Or even action this minute. She and Winston Churchill would have got on well together.

She dug into a number of molehills and poured paraffin into the tunnels. She covered them up again and came in, smiling.

'Now we'll see what happens,' she said.

What happened was that the moles immediately deserted the contaminated ground. But they started new heaps some distance away.

I said: 'Maybe you've got something.'

'What did I tell you!'

'But the damned things are still in the garden.'

'I know. But the line is now much nearer the wall.'

'H'm.'

I was seeing light. I took a spade and a can of paraffin and did a thorough job on every molehill still visible in my quarter-acre.

Again we waited. Part of the garden smelt like an old-fashioned ironmonger's shop.

The result was more successful than we had dared to hope. Instead of coming straight through the garden from the field to the spring, the moles now began to circle round it. Outside the walls heaps began to appear leading circuitously towards the shore. Obviously the moles had decided to avoid the smell of paraffin.

Since that day when Jean evolved a battle plan worthy of Churchill himself, we have had little trouble with the moles. Sometimes a small heap may appear in a remote corner of the garden – no doubt raised by a young adventurer who has failed to listen to advice from his elders – but a dribble of paraffin ensures that no more are added to it.

Jean is happy. So am I. And so, I believe, though their routes to the shore may be a few yards longer, are the 'wee moudiwarts'.

In spite of their depredations, which, after all, are on an infinitely smaller scale than those of human road-builders, it is difficult to dislike moles. In the underground dark, their natural environment, they are sturdy and strong. They work hard, morning and night. They raise families with faithful, busy intent and are considerate of their neighbours. Above ground they are blind and inept. With unnaturally large forepaws spread out as if in supplication, they lie helpless at the foot of a killer.

To avoid overcrowding and consequent 'aggro', each mole has its own lair and its own tunnel which leads to food and water. How, as they burrow in the darkness of the earth, do they recognize the near presence of other family tunnels and keep their distance? Perhaps the answer provides a clue as to why the smell of paraffin makes them change their routes. Perhaps they believe it to be the smell of an alien and dangerous human family.

It is an uneasy business, trying to live in harmony with nature. Not only for gardeners. For the birds and the rabbits and the moles as well.

7. Down to Earth

For many years, after returning in December 1945 from a five-year world tour at His Majesty's expense, I was more involved with writing (and with golf on the recreational side) than with gardening. This was necessary, because writing was my only source of income.

More than once, with a view to augmenting occasionally meagre rewards, Jean and I considered keeping hens and raising vegetables for the market. After all, since Jean's father was a farmer and my grandfather was a crofter in North Uist, we had a right to imagine that inherited instincts would serve us well. Something always turned up, however, which caused us to shelve the idea: a foreign sale of one of my books, a repeat of a Children's Hour radio serial or an offer from the *Glasgow Evening Citizen* for a series of 'country columns'. In the mid-fifties a Saturday night series of mine called 'The Glens of Glendale' became popular on Scottish radio; Jock went off to fend for himself, first on National Service, then as a sports writer with the *Daily Express*, and the county council loan on Achnamara was finally paid off. Our 'circumstances', as they used to be called in polite society, became comfortable enough and the vision of ourselves as part-time crofters was finally abandoned.

During all this time, while Jean continued quietly to propagate flowers and shrubs, I tried to grow vegetables for our own use. And I dug up a piece of ground in the shelter of the back wall in which we planted roses. But in those days, judging by the poor results achieved – except in regard to lettuces and parsley – I came to the conclusion that I was not born to be a gardener.

Sometimes, when in April and May a 'westlin' win'' blew

saft' and plentiful warm showers occurred, my potatoes would crop reasonably well and my turnips, carrots and cabbages, if they survived attacks by various pests, were of fair quality. But as a rule they were sorry specimens, the turnips hard as wood, the carrots minuscule and the cabbages incapable of forming heads. I failed altogether to grow onions and cauliflowers, and my peas were straggling, poverty-stricken disasters.

At this point, if they have read so far (which I doubt), expert gardeners will be laughing at me more heartily than ever. From the clues I have provided they will know exactly what was wrong with my garden and be eager to offer kind advice. But I beg of them to be patient: I am writing for inexpert people like myself and am intent upon presenting a background which for most of us is more realistic than the colourful pictures shown on seed packets. Also, being a storyteller, I am leading up to the entrance of the brilliant detective and a resolution of the problem.

As my golf handicap came down to 5, giving me enough exercise to keep a body healthy enough to contain what I, for one, believe to be a healthy mind, I am afraid I could dredge up no compelling interest in the garden. My failure to grow vegetable crops of even average quality I attributed to my own lack of skill. After all, my ground was similar to that cultivated successfully by villagers at Keil in days gone by – the same, in fact, as that cultivated by St Columba's monks fourteen hundred years ago. Maybe I lacked 'green fingers'. In any case, golf promised me much more creative satisfaction.

In 1974, when I became sixty-five, two blessings fell upon us. Jean and I accepted the old age pension, which allowed me to work at writing only in the mornings. And my boyhood friend, Robertson Finlayson, came to inspect Achnamara. The first meant that I could give more thought to gardening without it interfering with the golf, the second that I came under the influence of an expert chemist who was also an expert gardener.

Sixty years ago, when travel and hotels were relatively cheap, Southend was a favourite holiday place for young families. Farming was a depressed industry, with milk selling at only 3½d a gallon. Most of the farmers, therefore, in order to make ends meet, were eager to let rooms to summer visitors. There was also an excellent hotel of three-star quality.

Today the farmers are so prosperous (in spite of the Common Market) that there is no need for them to let rooms, though some, like our friends, Richard and Elizabeth, still do so, because they find pleasure in offering hospitality to strangers. There is still only one residential hotel. It is popular with maturer guests; but economic factors make it difficult for young families to use it in large numbers. Most of the children are to be found in the caravans which line the beach and in the bed and breakfast establishments.

Robertson Finlayson was one of the many boys and girls who spent July and August in the parish and joined our 'ploys' at the manse, in the heather glens and on the shore. I am of the opinion that he was probably the wickedest boy who ever made rude noises as an opponent prepared to hit a drive on the golf course or who gleefully swung long fronds of seaweed to whip screaming girls into the sea. The screams, I have to admit, were as much of pleasure as of pain or fear, an early indication, as far as I am concerned, of the complex nature of women. When I kicked Robertson's behind for being a nuisance, it was the girls who rallied immediately to his defence. A lifetime's experience has taught me that with women and gardens you can seldom claim a decisive victory.

But of course, when he controls the mischief continuously lurking behind his sharp eyes, Robertson has a nature kindlier than most. He surveyed my garden with what I can only describe as sympathy; and he refrained from uttering the sardonic comment which I knew was trembling on his lips.

'What you need,' he said, 'is a proper soil analysis.'

'For the garden?'

'Yes. You yourself may need analysis for various psychological reasons, but that is another story.'

'H'm. Then how do I go about it?'

'I've got the apparatus. I'll do it for you.'

Robertson had just retired after a successful business career. I knew, therefore, that the analysis I was going to get would be of a high standard. Having been brought up on 'natural' country lore, however, I was sceptical about the value of modern science as far as my garden was concerned.

I knew that the soil in my quarter-acre was essentially poor. It consisted mainly of sand heaped up on rocks which had once, centuries ago, been under the sea. But over the years I had tried to reinforce it with liberal quantities of farmyard dung and seaweed. And twice I had spread over it tons of good earth, one load from the manse garden when the Padre retired and part of it had been made into a car park, another from a new housing scheme in Campbeltown, ten miles away.

I imagined, too, that as its sandy base was plentifully mixed with seashell debris, it would contain plenty of lime, so necessary in the cultivation of most vegetables. When reading articles about gardening in the newspapers vague thoughts sometimes occurred to me concerning such chemical mysteries as nitrogen, phosphorus and potash. In fact, I had heard farmers describe the general fertilizer they used as being a mixture of nitrogen, phosphorus and potash in the respective proportions of 20 to 10 to 10. But I had always reckoned that all these were properly contained in dung and seaweed.

When Robertson eventually called to deliver his 'analysis' I received a nasty shock. It was brought home to me that I had been gardening for years in a haze of bucolic ignorance.

First of all he gave me a lecture about soil.

Until then, bothered as I was by strong winds, irregular sunshine, frosty nights, birds, rabbits, moles, carrot and onion fly, club root and a hundred other gremlins, I had given little thought to the actual soil in which I was working. This, I now realized, was ridiculous. Without soil there would be no plants at all; neither would there be any of the living creatures which prey on them. Soil, therefore, ought to be a gardener's most important study.

(I have pointed out to my publisher – and to various printers and booksellers – that here we have an analogy in regard to authorship. The author – or, more accurately, perhaps, the author's brain – is the soil out of which all the other jobs are created. Without authors would publishers, printers and booksellers exist at all? I am not sure if my idea is ever given serious thought. 'What would you do without the likes of me?'

I asked a printer once. He laughed, cynically: he had a new set of expensive golf clubs and was 3 up at the time. 'Print bingo tickets,' he said. 'And coupons for the pools.' Here may reside a clue as to why a printer's average weekly wage is rather more than three times that of an average author.)

Knowledge of the type of soil a gardener has to deal with, Robertson told me, is the mainspring of his success. Earth is composed of sand, clay and humus, and the amount of each in his garden dictates the kind of treatment it requires to produce crops of maximum quality and quantity. The ideal for garden-making, he pointed out, is a deep loam, free of all calcareous substances. (I did not interrupt to ask what the heck 'calcareous' meant; but I looked it up later, and apparently it refers to soil or water containing calcium carbonate or limestone. Which, at the time, didn't make me much the wiser.)

Deep loam of this nature, he went on, is extremely rare. Most gardeners, therefore, have to improve the soil that God has given them and grow in it those plants which by nature are best suited to it. That is, unless they want to emulate the professionals and use hothouses, special composts, 'grow-bags', fancy fertilizers, sprays and implements of every description. All of which (a) cost immense sums of money and (b) fail to give them the warm feeling that they have created something 'with the labours of their own hands'. (By permission of the Almighty, of course.)

Soil – like Gaul it seems – can be divided roughly into two types: sand and clay. Sand, by definition, is composed of 'fine particles of crushed or worn rocks containing no humus or earthy matter'. (I was encouraged by the thought that I knew what 'humus' meant, rotted dung and seaweed, dead vegetation of all kinds, dead worms and insects.) The large spaces between the particles of sand meant that a sandy soil holds air and therefore warmth, but not water. Clay, on the other hand, provides plant food and fertility; but the particles are so small and so tightly packed, leaving few air spaces, that in wet weather it becomes a sticky mass in which seeds fail to germinate.

'What kind of soil do you think you've got?' inquired Robertson.

'Sand,' I said.

'What kind of sand?'

'Just sand.'

'Acid or alkaline?'

I sighed. Things were getting more and more complicated. 'Why don't you tell me?' I said. 'You've got the answer in that soil-tester of yours. Anyway, what difference does it make?'

'A whole world of difference. Let me tell you.'

He was off again.

'Because of its lack of nutrients and because of its aridity – dryness to you,' Robertson quickly interpolated, 'sand has to be plentifully supplied with humus. It is also liable to severe leaching.'

'Leaching?'

'Yes. Over the years your vegetable garden has been leached badly. The rain has washed out most of the nitrates, so that your plants don't find enough nitrogen for their needs and grow sparse and stringy. Calcium and magnesium have been leached out, too. So have trace elements such as iron, aluminium and manganese.'

Metallurgy next, I thought. Was there no limit to this man's genius? Not only metallurgy: he had also presented me with a new word, 'leach', which I had always thought was spelt with two 'e's' and meant a bloodsucking worm.

I concealed my jealous admiration. 'I see,' I said.

He went on: 'There has been so much leaching, indeed, that your soil is now strongly acid, and we must do something about it. That is as far as your vegetables are concerned. Jean's flowers, her fuchsias, hydrangeas and veronicas – and these small conifers you have next the west wall – they grow well in acid ground, though they do need plenty of water and occasional applications of humus around their roots.'

'So all the good soil, all the dung and seaweed I've put into my vegetable patch have done no good at all?'

'On the contrary, you have done an excellent job in that direction.'

'Thank you,' I said. A new vision of gardening, utterly different from that indicated by homely advice gleaned from my parents and the likes of Old Alec was being limned before my eyes; and I was beginning to wonder if I had enough intelligence and strength of character to appreciate and accept it.

'But what you must remember,' he said, 'is that sand, unlike clay, contains no plant food and must be fed continuously, year after year, not only with humus but with artificial fertilizers as well: those which contain the nitrogen, calcium, magnesium, iron, aluminium and manganese which I've been talking about, along with other elements like potassium, phosphorus and potash. And while you have been building up the humus content quite capably, you seem to have overlooked the fact that your ground is acid and that lime as well as humus must be applied each year, because even in a few months it can be completely leached away.'

He saw that I was worried. He liked that. He laughed and resorted to satire. 'A man of your eminence in the literary world should have no difficulty in grasping what I mean and taking appropriate action. But as I am extremely friendly and forgiving – and have forgotten long ago all those kicks up the backside you used to give me – I have made out for you a written analysis, based on readings from my soil-tester. Each of the findings is accompanied by a recommended action, along with some advice on carrying it out. And I think I ought to do an analysis every year from now on, just to keep you right.'

'Robertson,' I said, 'you're a marvel!'

'A postscript,' he put in, quickly. 'And an important postscript at that. Never put lime on the plot in which you intend to grow potatoes.'

And because he is fond of quoting verse (and worse) – among his many attributes is a remarkable memory – he added in conclusion four lines, I believe by Abraham Cowley, an English poet of the seventeenth century.

> The thirsty earth soaks up the rain,
> And drinks and gapes for rain again.
> The plants suck in the earth, and are
> With constant drinking fresh and fair.

I thanked him, studied his analysis and did exactly as he told me, including the liming of my vegetable plots. Over the past few years the results have been remarkable. My cabbages are strong and healthy, my onions like footballs and my carrots much admired for their size and quality. I am happy in my gardening, secure in the knowledge that with Robertson's advice and encouragement my hard work will produce dividends.

Organic gardening? I still believe in it as an ideal. But in a pure and undiluted form it can only be practised successfully where the soil is perfect, neither porous or impacted, neither acid nor alkaline, and such soil is as difficult to find as gold in the Cairngorms.

Mine is acid and porous, and with the best will in the world I believe I should fail to make it viable without chemical aids.

It seems, however, that in a way I am fortunate that it *is* of sand. Sand is basically infertile and lacks the water-holding capacity of clay, yet it can be improved beyond all recognition by the continuous application of the humus contained in dung, seaweed and the compost midden along with balanced fertilizers and, where necessary, lime. But a garden of clay is different. V. Sackville-West, who gardened in clay and sand in turn, had this to say: 'Clay is a dire, plaguey, baleful, thankless soil, workable for about five days out of the year. My best advice to a gardener with clay soil is to remove your dwelling as speedily as possible to another place.'

Gardeners with sandy soil certainly have a further advantage. Digging in sand is easy compared with digging in clay. And the spade thrusts need not be so deep, because the humus will percolate down of its own accord.

And they can boast yet another silver lining. Sometimes in the late autumn and early winter, which is the most advantageous time to dig in the necessary dung, seaweed and compost, clay is so wet and sticky that it is unworkable. Sandy ground, on the other hand, is workable at most times of the year, so that gardeners can always have their ground ready for sowing and planting as early as the spring weather permits.

But gardeners in clay need not despair, as V. Sackville-West obviously did. With deep trenching and digging, good drainage and the appropriate use of chemicals based on annual soil tests, they can look forward to results which are happy enough, especially in regard to roses, strawberries and potatoes. But I doubt if they will be able to grow carrots as magnificent as mine.

Robertson's soil-tester is as much of a mystery to me as an X-ray machine: I will never be able to understand how it works. But I am prepared to trust his interpretation of its findings, just as I am prepared to trust my doctor's diagnosis. Robertson has cured my garden of its most serious defect, i.e. acid poverty. My doctor has cured me of mine, i.e. an acid gall bladder.

But even though I cannot tell how it works, I feel I must try to show what the soil-tester does. In short, it indicates the soil's pH value. A reading of pH 7.0, my mentor has taught me, means that the soil is neutral, i.e. neither acid nor alkaline. Above 7.0, it is alkaline; below, acid. The best value for most gardens, therefore is around 7.0. To make the soil more alkaline (as I have to do with mine) lime should be added; to make it more acid, sulphate of ammonia can bring about an improvement.

(Incidentally, if there is a hydrangea in your garden it may be used as a 'natural' soil-tester. If it produces blue flowers then your soil is acid. Pink flowers mean that your soil is alkaline.)

Here is an example of a recent Robertson Finlayson soil-test on my vegetable garden, with which he has incorporated the kindly advice which he knows is appreciated by someone like myself with a fairly low gardening IQ. For 'rotation of crops' purposes I have divided my plot into four sections, each of about nine square yards. They are indicated by the numbers along the top line.

Test	1	2	3	4	Action
	pH	pH	pH	pH	
Lime	6½	6	6¾	6	9lbs garden lime per 9 sq yards
Nitrogen	3%	3%	3%	3%	No action
Phosphorus	6%	6%	6%	6%	12oz bone meal per 9 sq yards
Potash	4%	8%	8%	8%	8oz sulphate of potash per 9 sq yards

Application

1. Dig in all manure at depth of one spade well before planting – at least three months.

2. Dress with lime two weeks before planting and rake or hoe in about 3 in. (Never apply lime directly on top of manure or artificial fertilizer.)

3. Dress in fertilizer (i.e. bone meal and potash) and rake in very lightly, about ½ in, the day before or the same day as planting.

4. A good fertilizer for use during the growing period can be made up from 4lbs sulphate of ammonia, 8lbs of bone meal and 4lbs of potash. These should be mixed thoroughly together and divided roughly into three parts. Apply first part fourteen days after planting, the second fourteen days later and the third fourteen days after that. The fertilizer should be sprinkled along seed bed or around plants. (Be sure to water well in dry weather.)

AND THE BEST OF BRITISH

So I take the action thus clearly explained; and, as I have said, the results are magic.

What does pH mean? I must admit I don't know, and I have never had the courage to ask Robertson about it.

8. As the Swift Seasons Roll

Gardening is like marriage. And, indeed, authorship. To ensure success you have to work at it continually and with love. There is no particular moment when, like Einstein with his theory, you can exclaim with a smile: 'Eureka, I've done it! Now I can sit back and laze in the sun.' As season follows season, as plants are either born or reborn, as they flourish in the warmth and then die or go into hibernation, you have to remain alert and vigorous, keeping pace with nature's rhythms and taking appropriate action to avoid its many hazards.

But, again like marriage and authorship, the end products of happiness and contentment are well worth the labour and the countless frustrations which occur along the way. Jean agrees with me in this, though as far as marriage is concerned she declares that her effort has been greater than mine. All I can say is that after nearly fifty years of experience she is entitled to her opinion.

Work in a sandy garden begins about the first week in November and ends on the thirty-first of October the following year; and I now propose to describe how it goes on at Achnamara. You may consider this a presumptuous exercise on the part of an amateur, but I can assure you that I have no desire to preach a gardening sermon – merely to indicate a trail that has led to pleasure and satisfaction in my own case.

Come to think of it, however, there may be an element of preaching in this whole book. After all, I am descended from a long line of preachers and teachers, as my name implies. But as an excuse for presumption – if an excuse be demanded by, say, a professional gardener who has continued to read – I once again call in as ally the old maestro, Will himself.

There is a history in all men's lives,
Figuring the nature of the times deceas'd,
The which observ'd, a man may prophesy,
With a near aim, of the main chance of things
As yet not come to life, which in their seeds
And weak beginnings lie intreasured.

And I also repeat what my father (the Padre) would often tell his parishioners: 'Do what I say, not necessarily what I do.'

In the winter months I collect and spread dung and seaweed and, on reasonably dry days, dig them in. This allows them to disintegrate and mix with the soil before seed sowing begins in the spring. Weather permitting, Jean also plants hardy shrubs, her most successful efforts in this line being fuchsias, weigelas, flowering currants and honeysuckle, all of which seem to appreciate our kind of acid soil and to live happily enough in our violent climate.

Note the word 'hardy'. Several times Jean has tried to grow certain ground-cover plants in her 'east' border, plants like rose of sharon and evening primrose. She selects them from a catalogue issued by a horticultural firm in the southeast of England which recommends November and December as suitable planting times. They seem to 'take' all right, but then, in our January gales and hailstorms, they usually wither and die, no doubt shocked by chill turbulence unknown in their nursery area.

Perhaps Old Alec's advice about seed potatoes should apply also to flowering plants. They should come from *north* of where they are to make a permanent home.

If you have a greenhouse, winter is the time when the seeds of various plants and vegetables can be sown in pots for planting outside three or four months later.

Greenhouses are expensive, so are the pots, so are the quantities you require of John Innes compost or Fison's Plant Grow. A do-it-yourself approach to this aspect of gardening is, therefore, much to be admired. In my experience, however, it seldom works. Yet I know some ladies in the parish, expert bulb-growers for the annual WRI Show, who have propagated flowers and some vegetables in their kitchens, using ordinary earth and compost from the garden and home-made seed boxes.

In a way, however, being a canny Scot without too much money in the bank, I can accept with a fair degree of equanimity the fact that a greenhouse at Achnamara is not, as the chartered accountants say, a viable proposition. Many years ago I tried to build a greenhouse against the east wall of the garage. Since our prevailing winds at the Mull of Kintyre come from the west I thought this might ensure its stability in a sheltered spot. Less than a week after its erection a cold and cruel gale blew in from the southeast. In one night of tempest my greenhouse disappeared in a shower of splintered wood and glass. Next day Jean and I decided that such a gardening luxury was not for us. From the wind – at the Mull of Kintyre – there is no hiding place.

(On that same night – in March 1946 – my friend the late Duncan Newlands, cox'n of the Campbeltown lifeboat, rescued fifty-four passengers and crew from the American Liberty ship, the *Byron Darnton*, which had gone aground on the Boiler Reef off Sanda, about two miles away from our front door. The remains of the *Byron Darnton*, like those of our greenhouse, now lie at the bottom of the sea.)

Our most persistent and evil enemy is the wind. Another of my winter jobs is the repair and maintenance of the windbreak which I have erected around the vegetable patch.

At the beginning the need for such a protection did not become immediately apparent. Then, on a certain weekend in June, a salty gale came raging in from the west. Tiles were stripped from our roof, and a litter bin was hurled over the wall, its contents scattered in all directions.

On the Sunday morning about a dozen empty whisky, gin and sherry bottles which had been thrown into the bin (after hoarding) for bulk disposal, lay in confusion on the lawn and around the front gate. Before I had a chance to collect them all we were visited by two young ladies from Campbeltown, members of a religious sect. They were obviously horrified by such evidence of what they imagined had been a night's debauchery and retreated quickly when I approached them with a bottle in my hand. But Jean and I made it to the kirk on time.

Real damage, however, had been done to my potatoes. Their shaws were blasted brown and broken. Young cabbages had been whirled round in the earth and uprooted. A row of dwarf peas, staked and tidy, were flattened. Veronica bushes and some hydrangeas were withered and scarred on the sides which had taken the full force of the gale.

I derived little comfort from what my father's old elder, Hugh McEachran, always used to say to me when weather caused an agricultural crisis: 'Look up the Book o' Genesis, boy. Chapter three, verse twenty-two.' I knew the verse well enough, having been taught it in Sunday School: 'While the earth remaineth, seedtime and harvest, and cold and heat, and summer and winter, and day and night shall not cease.'

But I have often wondered what, if anything, the writer of the Book of Genesis knew about gales.

I spent some time in the Middle East during World War II. Never once did I experience a high wind there, much less the kind of knockdown weather we get at the Mull. Indeed, I could well imagine Solomon's thoughts about wind (of the weather kind): 'Awake, O north wind; and come, thou south; blow upon my garden, that the spices thereof may flow out. Let my beloved come into his garden, and eat his pleasant fruits.' Would Solomon and the writer of the Book of Genesis have written in so poetic and serene a style had they lived in Kintyre. Sometimes when Jean is making soup, her beloved has to don waterproof trousers and an anorak to 'come into his garden' and dig up a few bedraggled carrots and parsnips for her.

Surveying the destruction wrought by that June gale, I made up my mind that the Almighty was trying to convey a message. For once He required assistance from me. So I invested in a long roll of Netlon small-mesh windbreak and set it up around the sides of the vegetable patch not sheltered by the wall. For its support I used a number of fencing stobs donated by farmer friends; and their real kindness may be understood when I remind you that ordinary wooden fencing stobs now cost more than £1 each.

The windbreak still stands. When winter gales tear parts of it to pieces I reinforce them with fresh netting which I keep in reserve. Other parts less seriously torn I repair with twine as a fisherman repairs his net. The twine I use is blue nylon, unravelled from a great hunk of rope which I found on the shore. (I told you: I am a canny Scot.)

The result is that the dark brown Netlon is now decorated with a mass of bright clusters which please my eye well enough but which sometimes encourages Jean and sundry visitors to remark that my vegetable garden looks like an urban slum. I smile in a superior way and invite them to have a look at the crops which flourish smugly behind it. And as an elder of the Kirk I quote to them a text: 'For the Lord seeth not as man seeth: for man looketh on the outward appearance, but the Lord looketh on the heart.'

Which no doubt makes them want to hit me on the head, because in Southend it is not the done thing to rubbish the Bible, especially that part of it written by the prophet Samuel.

As winter merges into early spring I can do certain jobs which would not be possible in, say, central or northeast Scotland, because the climate at the Mull – in spite of the wind – is comparatively mild and hard frosts are rare. (I have already suggested that the proximity of the Gulf Stream may have something to do with this.)

For example, moss on the lawn (and there's always plenty of that in lawns 'growin' in poverty') can be raked or even torn out by exasperated hands.

I once tried moss killer. It made a gruesome, black, sickly mess, and my lawn took several years to recover. I expect moss killer can be effective on lush, long-established lawns, but it may cause considerable damage if your garden is composed mainly of acid sand.

After getting rid of as much moss as manual labour can manage, I cover the bare patches with a mixture of earth, grass-seed and some kind of fertilizer like Fison's Evergreen. Results do not become apparent at once; but later on, as the sun rides higher, it is heart-warming to see how the brown and yellow blotches gradually disappear under a blanket of green. The Almighty never faileth, but I reckon you must give him a chance to work His miracles.

Early spring is also the time for manuring, hoeing and digging (with a graip) in Jean's borders, though this sometimes proves difficult when crocuses, daffodils and lilies are just about to flash their green. I think a small hand-fork is the answer for grubbing among bulbs. That – and plenty of love. And patience, which is the natural concomitant of love.

At this time, depending on the weather, I often plant some new mint (if the winter has been hard on the permanent crop) and a row or two of early potatoes.

The mint is for Jean, who insists upon it with roast lamb. She says she could eat mud with mint. I like it, too (mint, that is); but I have to confess that if given a choice I would rather have red currant jelly with my mutton.

The potatoes are planted in a spirit of bravado, in an attempt to steal a march on some of my neighbours, those otherwise friendly people who are determined that their Epicures, Sharpe's Express and Wiljas should appear above ground before mine. Occasionally, if the sun shines, my potatoes show quickly. More often they take their time, wisely remaining under cover if the skies are cloudy and cold. As a rule it may be said that it makes little difference whether potatoes are planted in early spring or later; in this part of the country, as I have said before, they will all be ready for eating around the first week of July.

I cultivate a 'nursery' bed which lies under a sheltering wall facing south. After long treatment it is now fairly rich in humus. In early spring I sow in it a variety of vegetable seeds which, with luck, are ready for transplanting in May or June. These include cabbage, cauliflower, kale, leeks and lettuce. I also use the 'nursery' to grow a few spring onions and early carrots. And a new clump of parsley every second year.

At the same time I plant onions and shallots in a heavily dunged part of the main garden (onions and shallots have hearty, even gross appetites), making sure that every bulb is dipped in a calomel paste as a precaution against the dreaded fly. I also sow some parsnips (Hollow Crown) – Jock says he could eat mud with parsnips – and the first of three successive rows of peas. These are always of the dwarf variety, on account of the wind. About this time, on a dry afternoon, Jean and I visit a small wood not far from Achnamara and collect sheaves of long twigs which, weeks later, I will use to stake my Meteors and Kelvedon Wonders.

Towards the end of March I usually notice weeds beginning to appear along the edges of the avenues and paths. This is my cue to buy two packets of Weedex and, using a watering can with a fine rose, to treat all my gravel with this invariably effective weedkiller. The results become apparent in about three weeks' time, when not a weed is to be seen anywhere among my gravel. The effect lasts for about a year, thus saving a great deal of work with the dutch hoe during the summer months – and offering more time for golf. To keep things tidy, however, the gravel needs its weekly rake after the lawn is mown.

At first Jean and I were worried in case Weedex might prove injurious to the birds and various animals which visit us. We soon discovered that our fears were groundless. The blackbirds, the thrushes, the wagtails, the house martins and the clamouring sparrows (or 'speouts' as we call them in Southend), along with Jason, the mongrel Labrador, Cara, the well-bred collie, and a variety of stray cats still give us their pleasant company. I should think the birds have enough sense to know where the poison lies and to avoid it when foraging for worms and grubs. Even human beings are wary of fishing in an area of sea polluted by nuclear waste. And the dogs and cats are fed at the back door, where Weedex is never used.

As spring slowly drags its feet towards summer the garden often looks drab, bare and uninviting. Jean and I begin to wonder if anything green will ever again show itself above the dull brown earth. Then one day we discover that the wind has gone, and the sun shines warmly on our backs. As if by magic weeds appear in the borders and in the vegetable plots. Daisies and dandelions poke up inquisitive heads on the lawn. Something stirs in our blood: a desire to 'fork and hoe, to plant and sow', which may be a kind of instinct inherited from our ancestors whose very lives depended on their ability to grow their own food. (Five-thousand-year-old-Neolithic chambered cairns are to be found all over Kintyre, greystone memorials to the first farmers and gardeners to inhabit the area. Carrot fly and onion fly would be unknown to them – as, indeed, would carrots and onions. But I am sure they had plenty of trouble with moles and with the wind.)

One fine day, however, does not necessarily herald summer. Jean and I are cautious. We observe weather signs and wait to see if the change to warmer weather is going to continue. (I sometimes use this 'trembling on the brink' day to mulch the roses with seaweed and to oil the lawn mower for imminent use. This I mention only in passing: my adventures with roses and lawn mowers will be mentioned in a later chapter.) But if the next day is also sunny we then go to work in earnest, weeding and hoeing first before sowing hardy annuals in the flower beds, including perhaps sweet william, wallflowers and canterbury bells, and main crops in the vegetable garden, such as carrots, turnips, beetroot and dwarf french beans.

If, by happy chance, the late April weather remains warm for several days, we continue faithfully weeding and hoeing. Then, perhaps on a Sunday before church, while doing my morning chores of bringing in coals and logs for the fire, I glance across at the 'nursery' and see faint lines of green. There is quick excitement. Jean is brought out to share it. The lettuce, the cabbage, the cauliflower and the spring onion seeds are showing through. The carrots and the leeks, therefore, cannot be far behind. And lo and behold, over in the main vegetable garden the first green potato shaw has appeared, thrusting up out of darkness to worship the sun.

We say our prayers of thankfulness in the church and, as the congregation 'skails' after the service, I seek out Margaret Cameron or 'Boskers' (Col. Hamish Taylor) or James Mac-Millan or Heather Dryden – who, as Robertson Finlayson's daughter, knows a thing or two about gardening – and ask, with assumed innocence and modesty: 'Your potatoes through yet?' More often than not the answer comes: 'Sure. Last Wednesday. What about yours?' But the chagrin is not too acute. I tell the truth and admit defeat once again. I know that we shall all be sitting down to our first meal of Epicures, Sharpe's Express or Wiljas on the last Sunday in June.

By tradition in Southend the last Sunday in June is when we hold Communion. Long ago, at the manse, my mother always arranged that after the service we should enjoy a memorable meal. It consisted of roast lamb, with mint sauce, peas and new potatoes from the garden, followed by curds and cream and stewed gooseberries, the latter also from the garden. The cream came from Donald Galbraith's farm, beside the church. A large, clotted jugful, sufficient to strain to the limit the gall bladders of every member of our eight-strong family, cost sixpence.

The appearance of the first green tinge in the 'nursery' plot is a signal. Now it is 'all go' at Achnamara. The lawn has to be mown, the roses tidied up (some useless growth may have been overlooked in the autumn pruning) and given a feed of an artificial fertilizer such as Rose Plus. More lettuce, peas, spring onions and early turnips have to be sown to maintain successive supplies.

I sow All the Year Round lettuce for early crops, Webb's Wonderful for a mainstay. Both develop beautiful, crunchy heads. My turnips are usually Purple Top Milan for first crops and Golden Ball for succession.

For a reason unknown to me I have never been able to grow swedes in my garden. Some kind of grub has always attacked them when I have tried. Jean finds this no great loss. There are plenty of swedes in the fields of Southend – for stock feed – and kindly farmers are always willing to supply her with as many as she wants during the winter months.

The farmers in Kintyre all pray for 'a dry May and a leaky June'. So do I. Such conditions make for bounteous crops in July and August. But in our sandy ground there is danger in dryness, too, and I make good use of the hose permanently attached (in summer) to the water tap outside the back door. I take the advice of the experts and do this at sundown, because water applied during warm, daylight hours quickly evaporates.

Weed, weed, weed. Hoe, hoe, hoe. (And mow, mow, mow.)

Early summer is also the time for lining the strawberry bed with straw or – a more modern practice – with torn up pieces of plastic. This is to prevent the fruit, when it comes, from being soiled and damaged by contact with the earth. When this is done I drape netting over it to foil the birds. For this operation I use eighteen-inch wooden posts capped with jam jars.

The jam jars ensure that the net can be drawn tightly without risk of tearing. You can buy (or make) wooden pegs to secure the netting to the ground. Crude, as always, I use large stones from the shore.

Other jobs at this time include thinning early turnips, transplanting lettuces and earthing up early potatoes. I don't know anybody else who does it, but I also put a mulch of fresh seaweed between the potato drills. My theory is that it maintains moisture in the earth. It certainly keeps the weeds down. In mid-May I give the carrot seedlings and the burgeoning onions and shallots a whiff of Gamma BHC. I am told this is when the first attack of fly may be expected. A second will occur at the beginning of July.

Weed, weed, weed. Hoe, hoe, hoe. (And mow, mow, mow.)

Jean has been busy with her flowers, planting bedding varieties like alyssum, aubrietia, nemesia, lobelia and antirrhinum, all of which seem to thrive in our kind of soil and can cower under the winds which will surely sweep over us later in the season.

She has been tidying up and lightly pruning, where necessary, the fuchsias, veronicas and flowering currants and cutting off the dead flower heads, particularly those of daffodils and lilies. 'Heading', we are told, allows the bulbs to hoard strength for the following spring. She has also been staking the taller perennials like poppies and foxgloves, piously hoping that no gale will occur in June or July to shatter their beauty once again.

And she has been waging war on the dreaded alstroemeria.

Alstroemeria is a strong and showy plant, popular with some housewives because when its orange-yellow flowers are cut they will last three weeks to a month in water. I believe its country of origin is Chile. But as far as Jean and I are concerned it is simply another gremlin in our garden, a science fiction horror.

It has trailing roots which burrow deep, almost a foot in some cases. They resemble pale, unhealthy worms and spread underground at frightening speed. One year your alstroemeria is confined to a small, nicely disciplined patch in the corner of the flowerbed. The next it has taken over the whole plot, strangling and suffocating all other plants which challenge its progress.

In early summer you make your first probing attacks, aimed principally at containment. The main assault will come in late autumn, when the flowers have died and the tough green foliage has begun to wilt. It is then that you dig out barrow-loads of the evil-looking roots and fork up the ground, adding a sprinkling of dung as you do so. It looks smooth, dark brown, purged of the obscene. In it you put a variety of ground-cover plants for the following season and wait in anticipation for an alstroemeria-free spring.

But inevitably you have left a few tiny pieces of the worm-like roots you have so savagely mauled. Every one of them proves fertile. During the first balmy days of March the whole plot sprouts alstroemeria and your delicate little periwinkles, dwarf geraniums, roses of sharon and lilies of the valley are smothered before they can become properly established.

It is like the Black Plague which fell upon the population of Southend in 1647, after the Siege of Dunaverty. Drastic measures had to be taken to counter that 'creeping death': clothes, household goods, even the houses themselves were burned. Our neighbour, 'Bill' Sayers, who, in spite of the name, is a lady – and about gardening, a very knowledgeable lady indeed – advises us that equally drastic measures must be taken against alstroemeria. 'Lethal doses of Tumbleweed,' she says, 'are the only answer. It means that your plot will be empty for a year. But in the end it will be worth it.'

Despite all this, Jean is always being asked for roots of alstroemeria by friends who admire its splendour when in full flower. She gives them away with pleasure but with a warning: a warning similar to that which she might give to an alcoholic begging for a drink.

9. Interlude: Concerning Alstroemeria

I pause and lean on my hoe.

One of the pleasures of having a garden is that you can work in it to a timetable of your own devising. Arguments about tea breaks and overtime do not occur – except, perhaps, when your wife's meal-time schedule does not quite harmonize with your own lazier rhythms. But, as a rule, as you labour to produce your flowers, there is plenty of time to smell them. And, maybe, to contemplate the joys and sorrows of the wider world, where ideals about loving your neighbour are so often unhappily ignored.

Plenty of time, too, to crunch a sweet young pea pod and light a cigarette. Especially when the sun shines and the wind dies and the great Rock of Dunaverty is reflected in the mirror of Machribeg Bay, a 9-iron shot from where I am standing. And when the scent of the honeysuckle comes delicately from behind the roses.

Jean is on her knees, grubbing away remorselessly at the alstroemeria. I am doing nothing physical except drawing on my cigarette, encouraged by the words of my doctor: 'Stop smoking? Of course you should. But you may consider it scarcely worth your while. Before you get all the nicotine out of your system you'll be over a hundred.' (This is one of the comforts of old age. The other is the fact that on the golf course you cannot drive far enough to get off the fairway and into trouble.)

I am letting my thoughts wander on to the subject of gardens and their relevance to life. Would the world not be a safer place, for example, if the Americans and the Russians channelled their aggression into growing bigger and tastier potatoes, rather than in manufacturing bigger and more lethal missiles? And if strident words in both West and East were uttered in more friendly and understanding tones.

Then, as Jean jerks up a long white root and, using a small swearword, hurls it over the wall, I am struck by the idea that alstroemeria is like bureaucracy. When it is allowed to spread, individual plants have no chance against it. I become aware of a slight rise in my blood pressure as I consider how miserably we have failed to curb the bureaucracy that has been creeping over our political garden.

With the growth of so many organizations, the size and power of the State has become frightening, as far as freedom-seeking individuals are concerned. Institutions, professional bodies, quangos, pressure groups riding on the backs of public relations hacks, all these are slowly but surely smothering individual enterprise and freedom.

The State now tries to classify us all under specific headings: trade unionists, members of the CBI, clergymen, doctors, lawyers, farmers, old age pensioners, single parent families, handicapped persons and so forth. If we do not fit into one of these institutional categories and can make no claim upon their powerful financial and moral support, we have to fight hard to establish our right to exist at all. Unless you are a member of a rich organization and are able, therefore, to persuade it to act for you, the protection of the law, in financial terms, is simply not open to you.

Recently I had dealings with a regional council about my rates. For a long time such dealings proved abortive because the bureaucrats could not understand that a self-employed, freelance author is unable to tell from one year's end to another how much he earns per week. It took months of patient explanation to convince them that my income is a feast and a famine affair: £100 for a newspaper article one week, nothing at all for the next two months, then a cheque for £500 for book royalties, more cheques for radio and television work and foreign book rights, followed soon by two or even three months of more financial drought.

In the end they agreed that a chartered accountant – at my expense – should provide them yearly with a statement of my income, *averaged into weekly amounts*. But I am sure they still regard me as a damned nuisance, resembling a spot of grit in their computers, who ought to be abolished in the interests of 'standardization'.

Government now is less the sovereignty of a benign ruler concerned with the common good, more the arbitrary rule of a despot doling out favours capriciously, always in its own interest. It is run like a commercial enterprise, in which individual interest is submerged in the pursuit of profit for the composite body. If this corporatism is not attacked and curtailed, as Jean and I attack the alstroemeria, it will certainly smother society in a dictatorship.

Dictatorship? I jab at a small weed among my onions and then lean again upon my hoe and light another cigarette. As yet Jean has not noticed my inactivity. I am able for a few minutes to consider how I may fashion my mental ramblings into a chapter for a book.

I know where they are leading me: into paths indicated by a re-reading of George Orwell's *1984*.

Orwell's vision of Winston Smith, the ordinary man broken and destroyed by Big Brother, should, I reckon, be like a whip on the flank of our laggard understanding, because it was people like Winston Smith – people like ourselves – who put Big Brother into power in the first place, allowing themselves to be seduced by visions of material riches presented in Technicolor by the propagandists.

It is difficult, of course, for ordinary people, some busily engaged in the urban scramble for existence, others with vision obscured by the mists of rural plenitude, to recognize and resist the blandishments of the false prophets who, in a twist of words and pictures, can turn murderers, train robbers, fraudulent financiers and drug-addicted musicians into global heroes. It is difficult to recognize and resist the carefully nurtured 'climates of opinion' in which applause becomes appropriate for amoral writers, film makers, business tycoons and politicians. As Cardinal Wolsey once remarked in another context: 'If the Crown were prosecutor and asserted it, juries would be found to bring in a verdict that Abel was the murderer of Cain.'

Into my mind come three statements made recently on

television. They have stuck like burrs on my conscience.

'It is not the business of an artist to make moral judgements.'

'The business man's first duty is to show a profit.'

'In politics there is no place for compassion.'

They sound sane and sensible enough (not unlike some advertisements for horticultural 'aids'), in tune with what we call 'modern sophisticated values'. But, upon logical analysis, they give me the same tremor of chill despair experienced by Winston Smith.

Some of the greatest artists who ever lived – Plato, Shakespeare, Michelangelo and Robert Burns among them – did not hesitate to issue moral messages which they believed might be of benefit to their fellow men. If an artist shirks the responsibility of making moral judgements, who then is going to make them? Big Brother?

If a business man says his first duty is to show a profit, it follows that his conscience must remain untroubled by the question, 'At whose expense?' Nor, in certain cases must he feel the slightest concern about people killed and maimed, people starving and riddled by disease, people on the rack of unemployment and poverty. It has not occurred to him that he is helping to create a 'climate of opinion' in which Big Brother can readily flourish.

'In politics there is no room for compassion.' These, I remember, were the words of a well-known elder statesman, a man who loudly declares his Christianity. (I seldom feel attracted to such 'holier than thou' characters.) They were uttered in general terms, bearing no relationship to any petty, passing scandal. I think it chilled me even more than did the others. The true meaning of 'politics', as distinct from 'party politics', indicates 'care for the well-being of the people'. If there is no compassion there can be no care, except in the sense that Big Brother 'cared' for Winston Smith.

The false prophets – the 'image' makers, the media propagandists, the leering gossip columnists who twist 'love' into a nasty, four letter word – are playing skilfully on our preoccupied minds, inflaming our material desires and denigrating our spiritual ideals as so much 'old hat'. What can be done to nullify their influence?

In the final resort, is the responsibility for changing and sweetening the 'climate of opinion' not ours, as individuals? It was I who prepared the plot. It was Jean who planted the alstroemeria. We were thinking at the time about the wonderful show it would make the following summer: a show which, with luck, would make our neighbours jealous.

So, as individuals, do we carry out our responsibility? Do we screech out messages of 'hate your neighbour' in sanctimonious, authoritarian voices which deny the divinity within every man? Or do we proclaim messages of 'love your neighbour' in voices honest and warm, with the laughter of spiritual joy behind them?

Surely we ought not to allow bureaucracy, like Big Brother, to do our thinking for us. Bureaucracy is not in the business of recognizing – and explaining to us – that the power behind a cruise missile is the same as that behind the opening petals of an alstroemeria plant.

My second cigarette is finished. I emerge, still leaning on my hoe, from a cloud of thought to find Jean, having finished her assault on the alstroemeria, regarding me without admiration.

'It's nearly five o'clock. If you don't hurry up you'll never finish that plot before tea-time.'

A hint of dictatorship there? Well, yes. But it is reassuring to know that you cannot get the sack for being idle in your own garden.

10. As the Swift Seasons Roll (continued)

Weed, weed, weed. Hoe, hoe, hoe. (And mow, mow, mow.)
The days lengthen, the heat strengthens, the ground at Achnamara becomes drier and drier.

> It haint no use to grumble and complane,
> It's just as cheap and easy to rejoice;
> When God sorts out the weather and sends rain,
> W'y, rain's my choice.

So said James Whitcombe Riley, in his 'Wet-Weather Folk'. And so say I, gardening many hundreds of miles farther north than the English poet did.

My vegetables and Jean's flowers and shrubs are all partial to heat. But they do better if there is plenty of rain to slake their thirst. Real growth in the garden occurs when, after a heavy shower, a thin, warm mist rises from the ground.

Old Alec had a word on the subject. 'I couldna dae withoot ma pint or two on a Sunday. Stands tae reason the wee plants is the same.'

Here, at the Mull of Kintyre, we seldom become victims of a drought. Nevertheless, a good hose is an important item in our otherwise fairly basic garden equipment. If the month of May is dry, as it often is in this part of the country, we use it frequently, so that young growth may continue without interruption. Peas, as the pods begin to form, and lettuce, before they begin to heart, are our thirstiest customers. Like sailors, they prefer their 'pints' when the sun has gone down below the yardarm.

In late May and early June, when transplanting lettuce, cabbages and cauliflowers – and thinnings turnips, carrots and beetroot – I try to keep my arid patch continuously moist. Always at the back of my mind is the old saying: 'A healthy plant is like a dog's nose – it doesn't look dry.' And if a north wind comes, adding cold to dryness, I also earth up the drills of young plants to keep them warm and less likely to be uprooted by gale force gusts. 'Keep sheuchin' them up,' is the advice I get from the farmers. But casualties do sometimes occur and replacements have to be taken from the nursery patch.

Transplanting is a tricky job, for which time and patience are needed. Some of my neighbours tell me I am too finicky about it; but I like to keep my young and tender plants as comfortable and happy as possible.

First of all, after sprinkling a general fertilizer and a little Bromophos over the ground into which I am going to put them, I lightly fork the earth, give it a good watering, line it off and make the dibble holes. Then I prepare a dish of calomel paste, use the watering can on the plants in the nursery and, with a small hand fork, dig them up, keeping as much earth around the roots as possible. Across in the main plot I dip each root in the calomel paste and dibble it quickly and firmly into the ground. Finally, like a nurse supplying a soothing drink to a patient who has just had an operation, I water the drills again.

Now is our last chance to sow for succession french beans, spring onions and some Purple Top Milan turnips. I have tried sowing peas in late June; but the crop has always been poor. This may have to do with the fact that in sandy ground, which loses warmth more quickly, the growing season is shorter than in a richer loam.

As the summer advances into July and August Jean's flowers are blooming and my vegetables have begun to offer bounty. The constant weeding and hoeing earlier in the season have paid dividends: the garden, now perfumed by honeysuckle, catmint and night-scented stock, is reasonably tidy. We can ease up on the hard labour for a spell and experience the pleasures of harvesting.

Jean collects roses, poppies and antirrhinums for her vases

and carnations for the buttonholes of certain of her friends. If the wind allowed she would also be cutting sweet peas; but anything over two feet high, of such a fragile nature, cannot be grown at Achnamara.

For my part I joyfully gather peas and carrots, shallots and parsley, turnips and early cabbage for the broth, lettuce, radishes and spring onions for the salad, mint and new potatoes for the roast lamb, strawberries, gooseberries and rhubarb for dessert.

What perhaps gives us most pleasure is that now we can make up small parcels of flowers, vegetables and fruit as presents for neighbours. Our motive for doing this may not be altogether altruistic: there could be about it a hint of boastfulness. And one-upmanship, if a neighbour's garden has been less than successful.

This is the time when Jean talks to her plants, berating them if they are less than eager to flower and complimenting those which are bursting enthusiastically into bloom.

She talks to everything: cats, dogs, birds, ferrets, worms, houseflies, even caterpillars. To the caterpillars – which she refuses to touch – she offers stern words. 'Very shortly a desperate man is going to find you. He will drown you in sea water or use a lethal spray. For your own good you had better scarper!' Later, when I announce a successful pogrom, she declares that her conscience is clear. 'I gave them warning,' she says. 'If they choose to ignore it, that's their fault.'

Talking to plants is commoner than some pragmatists believe. The closer to nature you get the more appropriate it seems to attempt this method of culture. When you tend a plant with loving care, nursing it, feeding it, watching it grow from a tender seedling into a strong and healthy flower or vegetable, you begin to experience a kind of affinity with it which induces speech. There is no doubt, of course, that the kinder you are to a plant the more likelihood there is that it will flourish and that you will be credited with having 'green fingers'.

But plants are like people: they do not always react to kindness. This is the time to talk severely to them and perhaps douse them with water to cool them off. Such treatment often works wonders. ('Water always works wonders,' is the professional's response.)

I know a lady in the south of England who, at one time, had cause to be angry with her cherry tree. For three successive summers it had refused to flower; and when a fourth spring arrived she decided to take strong measures. With a sharp knife she made a cut in the main stem – not far above the ground – and addressed it thus: 'Just a hint of what I intend to do if you don't flower this year! You're for the chop! And remember, I'm not fooling!' The result was miraculous. The tree produced a mass of flowers, the admiration of everyone in the village. And ever since it has continued to bloom in happy profusion.

An example of the efficacy of the 'short, sharp shock' treatment?

As summer slides down into autumn, there is again plenty of work to be done in the garden.

Spring cabbages, onions and winter spinach can be sown in the nursery bed for use early in the following year.

Plants must still be watered if there is any suggestion of drought. Leeks in particular ought to be given regular doses of liquid manure and, as growth continues, earthed up.

If new roses, shrubs and fruit trees are required, this is the time to plant them, when the soil is still warm.

By now potato flowers and shaws should be withering. It is a sign that the tubers underground are ready for lifting, drying and storing. Potatoes, I have discovered, keep best in hessian bags, tucked away in a dark corner of the garage. If exposed to light they become green and poisonous.

Main crop carrots can be lifted, too, and stored in sand. For this purpose I make use of plastic fish-boxes retrieved from the shore. With drainage holes in the bottom, they are also converted by some gardeners into seed trays for indoor use.

How so many of those fish-boxes are found on the beach below Achnamara I cannot explain. But obviously they come from passing trawlers and fishing-skiffs, washed overboard, it may be, in stormy weather, or flung into the sea by fishermen frustrated by capricious Common Market regulations.

Years ago I had an old friend nicknamed Angus the Bear,

who, even when ashore, always wore a lifebelt under his thick blue guernsey, which made him look like an advertisement for Michelin tyres. Wherever he went he was accompanied by an odour compounded of tar and chewing tobacco. When a night's fishing proved less than satisfactory, he was in the habit of hurling old wooden-type fish-boxes over the side of his skiff and roaring at an uncaring Government: 'Fucking bastards in London! That's whit I'd like tae dae wi' ye!'

It is too early yet to harvest beetroot and parsnips. In any case, I usually leave them in the ground to dig up as and when Jean demands them. We get so little frost by the seaside that they are unlikely to suffer winter damage. Indeed, our belief here in the country is that parsnips only reveal their true delicious flavour when nipped by frost.

In late autumn, before the equinoctial gales arrive, Jean plants tulips, crocuses, daffodils and other bulbs which she believes are necessary to augment her display in the following spring. She also transplants snowdrops, primroses and marigold roots. Shakespeare may have worked along the same lines. Remember the passage in *The Winter's Tale*?

> Daffodils,
> That come before the swallow dares, and take
> The winds of March with beauty; violets dim,
> But sweeter than the lids of Juno's eyes
> Or Cytherea's breath; pale primeroses,
> That die unmarried, ere they can behold
> Bright Phoebus in his strength – a malady
> Most incident to maids; bold oxlips and
> The crown imperial; lilies of all kinds,
> The flower-de-luce being one.

I do a variety of cleaning up jobs and pay some attention to the compost heap, which, by now, after being heaped with grass cuttings, vegetable leaves, potato peelings, tea leaves and other debris, has become large and bulging. I sprinkle on it a final dose of compost accelerator (such as Garotta) and give the pile a good watering. In another month or so it should have turned into a rich, dark brown mass. (Pea haulms, with their high nitrogen content, are particularly valuable ingredients.)

When Jean has picked the last of the roses, I hoe the rosebed and then water it with a solution of Jeyes Fluid. This, I find, keeps it almost entirely free of weeds for the next six months. Then I prune the standard roses lightly (along with the climbing roses at the front of the house), leaving the main pruning, which has to be severe, for the spring.

Then winter comes. Dung, seaweed and compost are spread on the vegetable patch – and on the rhubarb. I cease to mow. I dig and delve instead. Another season has started.

Then seek your job with thankfulness and work till further orders,
If it's only netting strawberries or killing slugs on borders;
And when your back stops aching and your hands begin to harden,
You will find yourself a partner in the Glory of the Garden.

It may be said by expert gardeners – and rightly said – that my choice of vegetables shows no flair, no spirit of adventure. In defence, may I point out that, lacking a greenhouse or even a cold frame (precluded from my plans, as the football managers say, because of the gales which harass the Mull of Kintyre), I have to confine myself to vegetables which can be grown and nurtured in the open, their only shelter a low wall and a tattered windbreak? Furthermore, since autumn growth slows down much earlier in my sandy patch than it does in richer soil, some interesting crops which I might sow later in the season – runner beans, for example – do not have time to reach maturity. Believe me, I have done my share of experimenting; but in the end I have settled for vegetables which I know from experience will do reasonably well in my particular garden.

Next year, however, after meeting with old friends from North Carolina – the Hunters – I propose to try a new exotic variety which they declare has a chance of being successful in the Scottish climate because of its quick growth.

I must confess that Jean and I had never heard of the squash, a close relation, it seems, of the common marrow. The Hunters tell us that it has a delicious flavour, not unlike that of a sweet potato. (Old soldiers who travelled in the East during World War II and found sweet potatoes all too frequently among their rations may question the validity of the word 'delicious'. 'Too bloody messy and too bloody sweet', was the verdict of one Scots Fusilier, accustomed as he was to the homely flavour of a Kerr's Pink grown in Ayrshire.)

As a rule our friends eat it raw in salads, though sometimes, cut into cubes, boiled in salted water and dressed with butter, it is enjoyed by them as a main vegetable.

The Hunters are descended from Scots ancestors who emigrated from Kintyre to North Carolina in the late eighteenth century; and it appears that the squash was much favoured by those early settlers because it could be grown in summer and stored easily for use over the winter.

Its apparent advantage, from our point of view, is that seeds sown out of doors in mid-June (when the ground has become warm enough to receive them) can produce a harvestable crop by the end of August (i.e. in ten weeks). They are said to require a sunny position and well enriched soil. I plan, therefore, to prepare the ground – as I would do for leeks – by digging trenches to the depth of a spade and filling them with dung, compost and soil to which has been added a handful or two of Growmore. Since squash grows on bush plants and needs a fair amount of space, I will then follow the Hunters' advice and sow a couple of seeds an inch deep every two feet along the drills. After germination in about a week's time I will remove the weaker seedling from each position.

I understand that like leeks – and Old Alec – squash appreciate their weekly 'pint', in their case of liquid manure.

Charles Hunter recommends a variety called Gold Nugget, so it is Gold Nugget seed that I will purchase. And for Jean's benefit Mrs Hunter has explained that squash are ideally used when they are small and tender, rather like courgettes, but that any we wish to keep for winter can be stored with safety in our cool, dry and frost-free loft, beside the onions.

I am keeping all this a secret from my neighbours. Imagine the smugness of my triumph if I can suddenly, with modest downcast eyes, present my rival gardeners with a succulent, exotic squash. I am also keeping it a secret because the chances are that in Achnamara garden the whole experiment will prove to be a failure, as so many of my previous ones have been.

11. Satyrs on My Lawn

They say it takes three hundred years to cultivate the perfect lawn. This may be true. The most beautiful lawns I have ever seen are within college precincts at Cambridge, and they are so old that nobody can tell me their exact age. Even more than three hundred years, it would seem.

I started my lawn about fifty years ago. It is still anything but perfect; but sometimes, immediately after a mowing on a moist summer evening, with the sun, low down over Keil Point, enhancing the pattern of stripes, a stranger with failing eyesight – and perhaps after having had a dram or two – may compliment me on it.

Near us, half a mile away along the shore, there lurks what appears to be an ancient ruin. This is Keil House, erected as recently as 1868 but gutted and partially destroyed by fire in December 1924. It was owned originally by James Nicol Fleming, a director of the City of Glasgow Bank, a fitting residence for one who had achieved great material success. At the entrance to the approach avenue he also built a lodge, on the roadside gable of which can still be seen an embossed rectangle of stone. On this, in due course, when ennobled by an admiring queen, he expected to engrave his coat of arms.

Unhappily, however, ten years after the building of Keil the City of Glasgow Bank failed, ruining thousands of small investors. James Fleming was arrested after attempting to escape from Keil House in a yacht which had suddenly appeared in the Bay and, along with his fellow directors, brought to trial. Instead of a luxurious country house with 365 windows, his home for the next few months was an urban jail.

To this day the rectangle of stone on the gable of the lodge remains blank.

In later years the House became a boarding school for boys, which, as Keil Technical School, grew and flourished until the disastrous fire caused the governors to transfer the whole establishment, under its original name, to Dumbarton.

What has all this got to do with lawns and gardens – apart, it may be, from a philosophical lesson concerning human vanity and blasted hopes? I am, in fact, leading up to a story told in Southend about the lawns laid out around Keil by Nicol Fleming.

The turf for their construction was brought at great expense from Ireland, and they made a green glory under a scrubby, sandy bank, which is actually part of a thirty thousand years old raised beach. This bank had always been infested by adders, the only poisonous snakes in Scotland, and people shunned it as a place of ill fame. But when the Irish turf arrived the adders suddenly deserted it, retreating into the heather-covered moors at the Mull.

Why such a quick exodus? Well, St Patrick, if you remember, put a curse on snakes, banishing them from Irish soil; and if spiritual blessings can be transferred from Ireland to Scotland, as happened in the case of St Columba, cannot curses be transferred too?

It sometimes occurs to me to speculate that if James Fleming had not imported Irish turf (and a curse on snakes) to Keil, my garden might now number adders among the many gremlins which invade it.

It has already been explained that when first sown with fescues, my infant lawn was denuded by a gale, most of the seed being deposited in a pile in our front porch. The resowing was not entirely successful. The fine fescues were soon dominated by coarser ryegrass, the seeds of which were blown in from the fields around us.

Years ago, when Jock was a boy – and his parents were more athletic than they are today – our lawn was kept in reasonable shape by the use of a hand mower. Jock and his school friends – and his father and uncles and various cousins – used it frequently as a football and cricket pitch. I also made it into a nine-hole pitch and putt golf course. (The gravelled avenue was deemed to be a burn, with a stroke and distance penalty for anyone who dumped his ball in it.) There was no question then of trying to turn our lawn into a smoothly striped work of art. Tufts of grass and dandelions sprouted in corners, traps for unwary golfers. Bare, deep ruts marked the creases at the wickets. Daisies grew on ground not trampled and scarred by footballers.

But some years after the war, when Jock and his contemporaries moved away to earn their living in urban areas, I decided to try and make a real lawn out of the Achnamara sports arena.

It was obvious, to begin with, that its bare and withered state would be improved by a good top dressing of earth. A load of this I was able to get from my friend George MacMillan, who was then the greenkeeper at Dunaverty, our local golf course. Sadly, George is now dead. He was the first child in Southend to be christened by my father. His grandson, also George, was the last. Old George's son, Willie, is now greenkeeper at Dunaverty, carrying on a notable tradition.

This top dressing, however, was of soil not unlike my own in sandy content, and, though it certainly filled up the ruts and the scars, I am doubtful if it did much to encourage the growth of new seed patches. But in a season or two, after some forking and the application of fertilizer, my lawn did begin to look more civilized.

At the time I had no expert to advise me about lawns. Jim McColl and George Barron, the Beechgrove gardeners on BBC Scotland, had not then begun their entertaining series, from which Jean and I have learned so much, not only about gardens but also about honesty and integrity in talking about gardens.

They appealed to us because of their humour and obvious joy in gardening and because they were always willing – unlike some other horticultural pundits on the media – to admit that they could make mistakes and that it was nature and not human ingenuity which always had the final say in the production of a prize-winning chrysanthemum or bunch of mint. They would also talk about flowers and vegetables without using the daunting Latin names which I, for one, have never been able to master.

As in music I can recognize the classical pieces and enjoy them, but there is no way I can remember their technical names, such as Etude No. 3 in B Flat major – or whatever.

Jean is better than I am at identifying flowers but admits to having been temporarily confused when an erudite neighbour asked her if she grew any Heuchera Sanguinea Brassingham Hybrids which are, in fact, coral flowers. Somebody once asked me if we grew Dianthus Barbutus. I said, 'No, unfortunately the climate at Achnamara does not favour such exotic plants.' He looked at me in such an oddly pitying way that when I got home I hurried to consult a grower's catalogue. There the truth was revealed. Dianthus Barbutus is the flower known to me as Sweet William, which can grow almost anywhere.

I wish Jim and George had been available many years ago to help me in the proper establishment of a lawn. They would have told me, for example, that on my type of sandy ground an annual top dressing is also a necessity and that such a top dressing should contain peat, compost and lime.

They would also have warned me that the installation of a sprinkler might be required, even in our usually damp climate. Recently, twice in four years, we suffered a drought in this part of the country, and I made the discovery that in only a week of dry sunshine – with, perhaps, a wind from the east – my lawn can become as brown and tatty as an old piece of cardboard.

One of these days, when I can afford it, I will buy a sprinkler. (It has just occurred to me that in the near future I may have collected enough coupons to purchase one cheaply from a cigarette manufacturer's catalogue.) In the meantime I rely on the frequent use of the hose to maintain a green tinge.

The question of expense is always worrying to an eager amateur like myself. Every week Jim and George (and now Dick Gardiner) show us new gardening aids, many of them labour-saving devices. Newspapers and magazines are filled with advertisements recommending products aimed at those of us who are bemused, bothered and bewildered by the constant struggle with nature. If I were a rich man – which, like Topol, fortunately for my peace of mind I am not – I should probably buy them all. But if I did, would our garden be such a pride and pleasure to us? Would our consciences not be affected by the suspicion that our flowers and vegetables might be acquired more cheaply in a shop?

To get real satisfaction out of a garden I reckon it is essential that you should cultivate your plants with as few artificial aids as possible. Jean's father and most of her ancestors were farmers in Ireland and Kintyre. My grandfather and most of my ancestors in North Uist were crofters. Their agricultural tools were primitive; fertilizers were supplied by their horses and cattle and by the gales which flung great glistening fronds of seaweed on to the shore. The production of crops on their sandy ground required from them a great deal of hard work, deftness and knowledge of weather lore, and I expect the genes we have inherited make us think and operate along the same lines.

I have a notion that a gardener who invests in the soil the work of his own head and hands rather than that of commercial firms eager for profit achieves more happiness in the end. He gets nearer to nature: nearer, perhaps, to God. Gardens are like people. They crave for understanding and individual treatment. Under the blanket rule of a Big Brother they tend to suffocate and lose their souls.

I do not mean, of course, that we should ignore the scientific progress which has been made in agriculture and horticulture. The farmers' fields and the village gardens are all in better shape because of it. And professionals gain richer rewards. But I would maintain that an amateur gardener derives the keenest pleasure from working with the minimum of tools, pesticides and artificial fertilizers; and if sometimes I envy the Beechgrove gardeners their batteries of modern aids, I have found it possible to produce satisfactory flowers and vegetables without them.

Our tools include nothing but the basic necessities. They comprise a spade (whose bottom edge, I am reminded, needs sharpening), a rake, a graip (Sassenachs call it a fork), a dutch hoe, a dibble (this came from the manse and is at least seventy years old), a small trowel, a little hand fork, a sheep-shears (presented to me after a needle match by my golfing friend Jim

McPhee and useful for edging the lawn) and last, but certainly not least, a lawn mower.

This mower, a two-stroke Atco, is, like its owner, geriatric. I bought it for £32 in 1954, when my thoughts were turning towards a lawn which looked more like a lawn and less like a neglected building site. At the beginning it was stubborn and temperamental. (Like a new wife?) Occasionally it would spring into life at the first pull of the rope. At other times half a Saturday morning might be spent in trying to get it started, and it would do so only after much fiddling with the carburettor and a constant drying of the plug in the flames of a forest of matches. I expect the trouble was that I had mixed too much oil with the petrol.

But over the years – and after much retrieving of the starter rope from the fields around Achnamara, where I used to hurl it in moments of stress – the mower and I have come to live together in a fair amount of harmony. The engine is now so old that it pants and wheezes – especially, like its owner, on a hot day – but it starts beautifully at the first or second attempt and, in spite of a chipped blade on the cutting cylinder, does a satisfactory job on the grass. I have learned, too, from trial and error, the exact amount of oil to put in the petrol. As it happens, this is not the same as that recommended by the manufacturers.

Another golfing friend, Duncan Watson, once gave me some excellent advice concerning a two-stroke mower. 'Always keep her well lubricated. And when you are finished mowing be sure to shut off the mixture and let the engine run until the carburettor is empty and stops of its own accord.' Nowadays I seldom see the ominous burst of blue smoke which means that the plug is being deluged by oily sludge.

I am always being told that I should buy a new mower. Pressure groups around me insist that I would do better with (a) a Flymo, (b) a rotatory mower on four wheels or (c) an electric mower. The arguments are as passionate and intense as those which assail an Energy Minister when he is considering – and, it appears, will continue to consider until time runs out – the respective merits of (a) coal, (b) oil and (c) nuclear fission. Advertisers litter the media with claims for new and better machines. I disregard them all, partly because most new models are priced beyond my means and partly because my ancient one still does a good job. I believe that my stripes are far more elegant than those made by any rotatory or electric mower. As for Flymos, they just cut grass and do nothing to achieve the artistic finish without which a lawn can only be described as a miniature field.

But mowing is not the only factor in the propagation of a good lawn. The elimination of weeds – particularly daisies – has got to be considered. Unless, of course, you are like Old Sammy, a former golfing partner of mine, who used to declare that greens with daisies were 'awfu' bonny', especially after he had sunk a long putt.

Or like the poet William Wordsworth, who had an inquisitive, not to say a moral theory about them.

> Small service is true service while it lasts:
> Of humblest friends, bright creature! scorn not one:
> The daisy, by the shadow that it casts,
> Protects the lingering dewdrop from the sun.

But then, lawn sprinklers were not invented in Wordsworth's time (1770–1850).

Nor were lawn mowers; though, as I have discovered, a gentleman from Stroud called Edwin Budding (sweet name for a gardener), who had become bored with his scythe, was experimenting as early as 1830 with 'machinery for the purpose of cropping or shearing the vegetable surface of lawns'. It is said that he got his idea from a machine used by tailors to cut the pile off cloth. It is also said that his engine looked like a clothes mangle standing on its head.

His original mower cost ten guineas and was sold to a zoo in Surrey. But poor Edwin failed to sell another until he reduced the price to seven guineas and advertised it as ideal for country gentlemen who would 'find in using the machine themselves an amusing, useful and healthful exercise'.

Amusing? Healthful? Had Edwin never heard of high blood pressure?

But we were considering daisies in a modern context: a

context in which they are deemed to be unsightly. (Except in 'fields where lovers lie' and weave their dreams into daisy chains.)

There are plenty of good selective weedkillers on the market; but I have found, in my case, that the best is Mecadex, a large container of which I was able to buy wholesale through the good offices of the Dunaverty Golf Club. An application of Mecadex in April ensures that my lawn is comparatively weed free all summer.

But even Mecadex is not guaranteed to kill daisies; and so, a number of years ago, I decided that the best way of ridding my lawn of those 'flowers in the wrong places' was to dig them up. It seemed a daunting task, considering the area of grass which they infested; but as a writer of books, accustomed to long spells of painstaking work before a job is done, I faced up to it with resignation and all the determination an essentially lazy Hebridean could summon to his aid.

With string I divided the lawn into long, yard-wide strips. Using a little two-pronged fork and on my knees, I patiently dug out every daisy in each strip before going on to the next. It took me several evenings in a warm, moist June to complete the job. But when it was done I felt the same glow of relief and satisfaction which always comes to me on writing 'The End' beneath the last paragraph of the final chapter.

And it was the end for the daisies on my lawn. Now, when one appears to sully the green, it is the work of only a moment to find the little fork in the garage and deal out death.

After writing the foregoing paragraphs I was discussing weedkillers with Willie MacMillan, identified previously as our greenkeeper at Dunaverty. He told me that Mecadex has now been taken off the market. I wonder if, like the bodywork of some old cars, it proved to be so good that it inhibited the sales of new products? Or am I being unfair to earnest and innocent commercial interests?

There are, of course, other gremlins which can make a lawn unsightly. I am in a position to testify that one of the deadliest is a herd of cows.

One Lammas Fair evening Jean and I attended a concert in

the village hall. When we went in the August evening was beautiful. When we came out it was raining so heavily that the puddles in the road, under the headlights, looked like spiked golf shoes turned upside down. (At the Mull of Kintyre the 'Lammas Floods' are notorious phenomena, resembling monsoons in India: fine for gardeners but the bane of golfers and sports promoters.) I turned the car into the avenue at Achnamara and ran it quickly into the garage.

'Make a dash for the back door,' I said to Jean. 'And I'll be on your heels. I'm damned if I'm going back down to close the front gate in this downpour!'

Early next morning we awoke to an outlandish sound: a sound so loud and mournful that it might have been the death rattle of a dinosaur. I jerked upright in my bed. The sound had been startlingly close, almost in my ear. At the open window, as a further shock, I saw a large cow looking in, mooing as if in agony.

I threw off the bedclothes and leapt out. Rushing from room to room I found that the back green, the front green, the vegetable garden and the flower plots were crammed with cows. They looked lost and forlorn, but scarcely so lost and forlorn as the garden. Into the wet turf and open soil their feet had sunk to horrific depths and now, as they milled about, they were destroying flowers and vegetables before my eyes.

I may have screamed.

I thrust on my slippers, unlocked the back door and ran outside, shouting every swearword that a minister's son and a former member of Her Majesty's Forces could remember. (Which were not a few.) Nightmare lines written by Christopher Marlowe crept into my fevered brain.

> My men, like satyrs grazing on the lawns,
> Shall with their goat feet dance an antic hay.

My pyjamas were a bright maroon, a colour chosen, much to Jean's distress, because I am a supporter of Motherwell Football Club. This seemed to attract the cows rather than repel them ('red rags to a bull'?); but eventually I was able to direct the 'lowing herd' towards the open front gate. As it 'wound slowly o'er the lea' (i.e. my front lawn) cloven hooves sank even deeper as cows jostled and pushed and leapt upon each other to escape the maroon madman behind them. The noise was louder than in a stockyard. Cowpats proliferated on grass and gravel. The smell became hideous.

At last I got most of the herd – numbering, if memory serves, some hundred beasts – out through the gate and on to the road. But then, as in an X-certificate film, horror was piled on horror. A builder's heavy lorry containing gravel from the shore came thundering along on a collision course with the cows. The driver stamped on his brakes and blew his horn. The cows turned and, by now scared out of their senses (if cows do have any sense, which I doubt), came stampeding back into my garden. I had to jump aside to avoid being trampled to death.

The lorry went on its way, the driver waving cheerily, as if to a friend, apparently unmoved by my desperate appearance and by the varied descriptions of his parentage which I shouted at him.

It was another ten minutes before the cows were on the road again. I shut the gate. About two hundred yards away I saw a hole in the fence through which, stupid and blinded by the rain, they had come in the night. But I had no intention of driving them back through it. Someone else – hopefully the farmer himself – could look after the beasts from now on. And motorists and lorry drivers could get stuck among the herd for all I cared. Loving your neighbour is all very well in theory, but circumstances alter cases. I had the rehabilitation of my lawn and garden to attend to. I had to put on some clothes and eat a breakfast which would taste like sawdust.

Jean said: 'A Saturday, too. You'll miss your golf.'

'I know!' I said and clenched my teeth on further comment. It was not a time for words.

From eight o'clock in the morning until about seven that evening we laboured to prise up the hoofmarks and level them off with topsoil. Dusk was falling before the rows of peas and cabbages and turnips were repaired and given the kiss of life with sulphate of ammonia. Word was brought to me that my mower man, Duncan Watson, had won the August medal and qualified for the finals, a feat which I had hoped to achieve for myself that day.

At about ten o'clock, after a revitalizing curry, Jean raised her delicate Martini. 'Here's to rural peace!' she said.

We felt as Hillary and Tensing must have felt on the peak of Everest, sore and exhausted but happy in achievement. 'That'll be the day!' I said. But the glass of Dewar's tasted good all the same.

And, such is the healing genius of nature, in less than a week almost all traces of bovine invasion had vanished in the greenness of new growth.

A precious load had also been added to our dung-heap.

Another gremlin with which we had to contend was a horse: a pony belonging to Jean's cousins who used to host the Keil Hotel built on the raised beach behind us.

His name was Cruachan (which is the name of the highest mountain in Argyll and also the battle cry of the Clan Campbell), and Jean soon became his dearest friend, feeding him with carrots, lettuces, cabbages and other vegetables which, in view of his burliness and shining health, I felt might have been put to better use. Feeding the poor, for example, among whom I always include authors and their wives.

It began with Jean's siren calls to him – 'Cruachan! Come on, Cruachan darling!' – as he grazed in the field at the back of the garden. And there she would stand at the wall, waving a carrot or a cabbage, and he would come trotting to her, uttering small neighs of pleasure. While he munched luxuriously, she would talk to him and he would nod his head in understanding. If I were working in the garden I would make rude remarks about him, which he – and Jean – always ignored.

Inevitably, as time went on, Cruachan no longer waited for a call. He had noticed, during his love-ins, that vegetables and roses grew just over the wall: a wall only four feet high over which he could stretch his neck. Once or twice I found him nibbling enjoyably at carrot-tops and rosebuds and hustled him away with rude and violent gestures.

Finally, full of cunning, he would wait until we had gone off somewhere in the car and then, at leisure, pull the carrots and roses right out of the ground.

Our next-door neighbours' garden was similarly assaulted by him. They retaliated by erecting a high wire fence on top of their wall. Which only meant, of course, that he came to us even more often.

In the end Jean was forced to give him a cuff on the ear (which would not have injured a butterfly) and treat him to a severe lecture, after which, to my despair, she patted his nose, uttering words of comfort. 'He's promised never to do it again,' she told me.

And, surprisingly, neither he did, though Jean still continued to feed him on my precious carrots.

I was helpless in the situation. It was our son who found a way to ease the strain.

One autumn evening, as Jean and Jock (who is as daft as his mother about animals and birds) were conversing with Cruachan over the wall, no carrots happened to be available for his 'tasty bite'. (I had lifted the crop before he could eat it all and stored it away in a secret, sand-filled fish-box.) Jock, however, had a peppermint in his pocket, of an extremely hot variety. This he offered to Cruachan, who took it gladly and began to crunch.

All at once a glazed expression appeared in his eyes. His head went up. His long tongue emerged. He began to wheeze. The tongue moved in and out again, more and more quickly as it sought cooling air. Jean and Jock became anxious. I began to laugh.

Cruachan was grievously insulted. He gave Jean and Jock a look of reproach, shook his head vigorously, snorted, then turned and raced away across the field, kicking his heels behind him.

It was a long time before Jean saw him again by the wall, but finally he did come back. Just as they were re-establishing relations, however, suspicions dying on both sides, his owners retired from the hotel and took him away to live in another part of the parish.

Our roses and carrots now grow in comparative safety. The young cattle in the field are not so friendly; and, at any rate, they are never there long enough to discover the delights available if they stretched their necks over the wall.

12. Old Wives' Tales

My grandmother on my mother's side, *née* Mary Cameron from Appin in North Argyll, was a great one for what she called 'natural medicine'. I only saw her once, when I was about nine years old; but I retain a picture of a sedate old lady wearing a mutch (the frilled white cap fashionable around the turn of the century among elderly Scots country-women) and singing softly in the Gaelic as she worked at her spinning wheel.

Her husband, Archibald MacKenzie, was a sheep-farmer, with a flowing grey beard like that of Abraham in our illustrated family Bible. He was often troubled by indigestion, but this was always successfully eased by my grandmother's concoctions. The Padre, who liked to pose as a realist when the mood was on him, used to annoy my mother by hinting that her father's stomach pains were the result of too much 'natural medicine'. Be that as it may, it seems to have done Archibald no serious harm, because he lived until he was nearly ninety. (The Padre depended mainly on Bismuth powder in a glass of milk to allay nervous, prepreaching stomach twinges on a Sabbath morning. He lived even longer, until he was ninety-two.)

My mother inherited some of the Cameron beliefs in the medicinal properties of plants. We always accepted the wisdom of 'what granny used to say' with some scepticism; but when I became interested in vegetable gardening and began to read books on the subject it surprised me to discover that many of her beliefs were obviously derived from cultures even more ancient than that of Scotland.

The practice of 'natural medicine' has a documented history dating back at least to *c*. 320 BC when Theophrastus wrote his *Enquiry into Plants*. Pre-Christian Roman authors supply evidence regarding the potency of certain herbs, notably the fennel which was chewed by gladiators to increase their bravery in the arena. (There's mint in some brands of chewing gum. In the future, therefore, historians may speculate that twentieth-century footballers used it to increase their bravery at Hampden Park or Wembley.) And in Britain whole libraries of books have been written on the subject, among them Boorde's *Dyetary* published in 1542, Parkinson's *Paradisi in Sole, Paradisus Terrestris* (1629), John Evelyn's *Aceteria, a Discourse on Sallots* (1699) and, in modern times, John Seymour's *Gardener's Delight*, published in 1978, a book which, in my opinion, offers delight not only to gardeners.

Recently the World Health Organisation has become interested in 'natural medicine' and has ventured an opinion that the practice of orthodox medicine might benefit by a return to the act of 'simpling, which is neither base nor contemptible, but an exercise for the noblest'.

It has been estimated that this investigation into herbal remedies will take about ten years before its recommendations, dosages, indications and *materia medica* are in the hands of general practitioners. I suspect that such an estimate may be too optimistic. Official studies always tend to be 'blate' (tardy), as we say in Scotland.

In any case, I wonder if the World Health Organisation realizes that much of the groundwork for its research was done four hundred years ago by John Gerard of Nantwich, who was 'assistant to one of the chirurgeons-in-ordinary to Queen Elizabeth'.

Gerard collected herbs as a philatelist collects stamps. In his garden he grew more than a thousand of them, native and foreign. Being under royal patronage, it is possible that he prescribed for the ulcers acquired by Sir Francis Walsingham in his stressful job as spymaster-in-chief and head of Queen Elizabeth's version of MI5.

I should not be surprised either if it was from him that Shakespeare acquired all the detailed herb lore with which his plays are sprinkled. Or could the reverse be true? Did Gerard employ the popular playwright to incorporate in his stage shows a few subtle 'commercials' to promote his products?

(Shakespeare was a professional, always willing to turn his pen to any kind of writing in quest of an honest penny. I have a notion, indeed, that he was one of the original translators of the Bible. If it wasn't Shakespeare who wrote the thirteenth chapter of I Corinthians, then it was someone of equal genius as a writer: someone whose existence has yet to be established.)

In 1597 Gerard published a book called *Herbal*. In the introduction he writes: 'No confection of the apothecaries can equal their [herbs] excellent virtue. . . . The hidden virtue of them is that the very brute beasts have found it out.'

I am told that the World Health Organisation is especially interested in willow leaves, which, it has been found, provide an effect similar to aspirin. Gerard says that with a slight modification in the distilling process they can also be used to 'drive away serpents, ants and gnats, and as a yellow hair dye'. (Queen Elizabeth had trouble with her hair. Did she consult him about it?)

It occurs to me that Gerard, like most advocates of 'natural medicine' before and after his time (including my granny from Appin), is liable to get carried away by his enthusiam and to build tall castles on shaky foundations. Having proved by experience that a plant has one particular healing virtue, he then goes on to claim for it a number of other virtues which can only be described – in a kindly way – as theoretical.

Consider, for example, what he says about the common onion. Sniffing its juice up the nose 'purgeth the head and draweth forth raw phlegmatic humors'. Well, of course it does, as any gardener or housewife can testify: especially any gardener or housewife who lives at the Mull of Kintyre, where catarrh is endemic. But then, setting Pelion on top of 'leafy Olympus', he proceeds to declare that when 'crushed with salt, rue and honey' onions are good against the biting of a mad dog and that the pure juice, 'rubbed upon a bald head in sunlight bringeth the hair again very speedily'. (I suggested the latter experiment to a friend of mine who is so bald that his head shines even in the dark. 'Does it heck!' was his reply. 'I tried it. And nearly got sunstroke!')

Some of Gerard's 'cures' are, I suspect, based on false premises. Either that, or he is indulging in some deadpan humour at his patrons' expense. He says that lily of the valley, distilled with wine, restores speech 'to them that are struck dumb'. And that borage, when the leaves and flowers are dunked with wine, 'maketh men glad and merry, driving away all sadness, dulness and melancholy'. But is it the herbs or the wine that doeth the trick? I reckon Old John enjoyed many a convivial evening demonstrating his 'cure' to friends and acquaintances – irritatingly silent men among them – willing to pay the wine bill.

Gerard also claimed that rhubarb, mixed with liquorice and boiled in beer, purifies the blood and 'maketh young wenches look fair and cherry-like'. Sober analysis would seem to indicate that in this case the true herbal mystique is missing. Such a mixture would cause anybody's bowels to move, resulting in a surge of good health exemplified by cheeks 'fair and cherry-like'. A couple of Beecham's pills would do the same, with much less trouble.

There is one vegetable, however, for which Gerard had no regard: the Jerusalem artichoke. 'In my judgement,' he declared, 'which way soever they are dressed and eaten, they are meat more fit for swine than men.' I agree with him. (And I would say the same about courgettes, if I dared.)

It will be interesting to learn if the World Health Organisation finds any virtue in an artichoke's knobbly knees. (Or in a courgette's bland tastelessness.)

Throughout the centuries the therapeutic properties of various plants have been the subject of experiment by herbalists of every clime and creed. If the World Health Organisation pays any attention to all that has been written about 'natural medicine' it may experience the same dither of doubt in which I find myself. But then it may not. I have no computer, no means of discovering common denominators in a scientific fashion. The World Health Organisation has all these aids.

What follows are odds and ends of plant lore which I have gathered from grandparents, parents, friends and books. I don't believe in all of them; but at the same time it is interesting to speculate on possibilities. And in them, as in the folklore of my Hebridean ancestors, there may exist somewhere a few grains of truth.

13. 'A Vegetable Love'

Here I will confine myself to vegetables which I actually grow in my garden. And in an effort to appear methodical and scientific – which will probably fool nobody – I present them in alphabetical order.

Beetroot

Nicholas Culpeper (1616–54) tells his readers that the juice of the white beet 'openeth obstructions both of the liver and the spleen' and is good for headaches. The juice of the red beet, he says, 'purgeth the Head, helpeth the noise in the Ears'. (What all this sniffing up the nose might do for my tender sinuses I can only imagine.)

My granny used to say that eating raw beetroot (every day) prevents cancer.

All I know is that a neighbour of ours makes marvellous soup out of it, on the lines of the Russian *bortsch*. And that Jean uses it to create a delicious chutney which we enjoy in the late spring when other vegetables are scarce.

I asked Jean to give me the recipe for her beetroot chutney, so that I might pass it on.

'I can't do that,' she said. 'I do it out of my head.' (She plays the piano by ear as well, beautifully.)

Which reminded me of the time I asked a Hebridean relative of my own, renowned for the quality and potency of his home-made Atholl Brose, if he would let me into his secret. 'Och, there's no secret about it,' he said. 'I just take whisky, oatmeal, honey and cream and bugger them all up together.' (But he omitted to tell me the exact quantities.)

I repeated this story to Jean and said: 'All right, I'll just say you put in such and such and such of such and bugger them all up together.'

She was scandalized. 'You will not! If you're going to mention my chutney at all I'll give you a proper recipe. But I can't guarantee it will work out for other people as well as it does for me.'

Here it is.

2 lbs cooked beetroot, 2 lbs apples peeled and cored, 1 lb onions, $\frac{1}{2}$ lb sugar, $\frac{1}{2}$ lb raisins, $\frac{1}{2}$ lb sultanas, 2 teaspoons ground ginger, 2 teaspoons ground cinnamon, 1 tablespoon salt, 1 pint vinegar. Dice beetroot and put in a large basin. Cook apples and onions in vinegar. Add fruit, spices, salt and sugar and cook a little longer. When cool add to beetroot. Mix thoroughly and store in jars.

Beetroots grow well in my sandy garden, with plenty of dung to nourish them. I treat the ground with lime and potash and sow the seed thinly, for succession. Nowadays I never sow my first batch until about the end of April or the beginning of May. At one time, with greed for earliness, I did so at the end of March. The beetroot grew all right, but most of the crop tended to bolt. I have found that later sowing prevents this.

As far as I am concerned the cultivation of beetroot is easy. Only lettuce gives me less worry. Gremlins seem to ignore it and even bad weather has no ill effects. I have left beetroot in the ground throughout the winter and, in the spring, still found the roots tender and tasty.

Two things, however, ought to be remembered. Beetroot leaves should be twisted off, not cut, in order to prevent loss of juice. And, according to my mentors, they should never be put on the compost heap. There is a scientific explanation for this; but, as you know, my education in that direction is meagre.

Brussels Sprouts

Where the name 'Brussels' comes from is to me something of a mystery. A romantic explanation is that Julius Caesar brought the plant to Belgium from its natural habitat in the Mediterranean area and that the Belgians, in later years, exported it to Britain.

I have found brussels sprouts difficult to cultivate, not because they are delicate – they are, indeed, extremely hardy – but mainly because they grow tall, and anything tall in my garden is liable to destruction by salty gales roaring in from the Atlantic. They can, of course, be staked; but even stakes may be flattened in our kind of weather.

In addition, sandy ground is not ideal for them, though I have found they can be grown satisfactorily when the sand is reinforced by plenty of dung, seaweed and compost. Another disadvantage is that in order to ensure good sprouts the soil must be firm, which is always difficult to achieve on sand.

Brussels sprouts are also liable to be attacked by two gremlins which are the particular bane of all brassicas: club root and cabbage root fly. My experience is that a liberal use of lime in January or February (bringing the soil to a pH of a little over the 7 recommended by Robertson Finlayson) and an application of calomel dust when planting out can do a lot to prevent club root. Bromophos scattered round the young plants may, with luck, be enough to scare away the root fly.

An important factor in the prevention of these two pests would seem to be a constant rotation of all brassica crops.

My mother always insisted that the sprouts, once they begin to grow, should be picked upwards along the stem. She used to pick off the plant tops (before the New Year when they began to seed) and offer them to us instead of cabbage. We seldom spotted the difference.

Jean tells me that she cooks sprouts in salty water, taking them out before they become soft. For the benefit of those not troubled by weight or gall-bladder problems, she adds: 'Brussels sprouts are delicious when parboiled and then roasted with the meat or tossed in boiling fat.'

Cabbage

'Cabbages are extremely windy, whether you take them as Meat or as Medicine; yea, as windy Meat as can be eaten, unless you eat Bagpipes or Bellows, and they are but seldom eaten in our Days.' So said our friend, Nicholas Culpeper, lapsing into a rare bout of humour.

But he was surely in a minority among herbalists in thus denigrating the health-giving properties of the humble cabbage. (Was he something of a snob as well as being anti-bagpipes?) The ancient Egyptians not only ate the cabbage, they also worshipped it. In more recent times it has been called 'the doctor of the poor, the medicine that is the gift of Heaven'. And our grandmothers, including mine and Jean Palaiseul's (*vide* her book, *Grandmother's Secrets*, published in 1973), believed it had a multitude of therapeutic properties.

For example, a concentrated concoction of five or six leaves to a litre of water, boiled for half an hour and sweetened with honey, was their remedy for all bronchial afflictions; and a jelly procured by boiling cabbage leaves in milk was supposed to cure lumbago when applied in a poultice.

Recently I was told that my granny used the heart of a cabbage, cut in half and wielded like a brush, to clean and renovate her carpets.

'Whaur's yer expensive shampoos noo?' I said to Jean.

She looked at me with her usual patience and pity. 'A little vinegar in the water does much better,' she told me. 'And it's not so messy.'

Cabbages always seem to do well in a sandy garden, provided the ground is properly prepared and all necessary precautions taken against brassica pests. They like well-manured soil, with plenty of nitrogen in any 'artificials' used. When growing, if the weather is dry, they will drink up as much water as you can give them.

I sow the seed in my 'nursery' in early March and transfer the plants to the main garden in May, using plenty of water. They are ready for use in July, August and September. Lucky people with a sheltered garden can also grow winter varieties by sowing in May and planting in July. They mature in December.

I must say I love cabbage, when it is cooked crisply by Jean. And yes, I love it especially with corned beef.

Carrots

Jean has a passion for carrots. Carrots, therefore, are now a main crop in the garden, even more important in the scheme of things than onions and early potatoes.

It is fortunate that my sandy ground is ideal for their cultivation. All the experts agree that they grow best in light soil, well dunged from a previous crop such as lettuce or peas.

Something I have learned is that fresh dung tends to make them fork.

For long I struggled to subdue their most evil enemy, the carrot fly. But by the use originally of Gamma BHC and then, later, of Bromophos (following the example of the Beechgrove gardeners), I now seem to have gained a victory. Constant vigilance is still maintained. With neighbours always complaining of devastated crops, I am aware that at any moment the enemy may strike again.

Some of my friends grow them in beds, which would seem to be a logical idea for the early 'finger' types – so sweet and tender – which do not require much thinning. (There is a local theory that thinning lets in the carrot fly. I am doubtful about this. In any case, I always insure against the possibility by investing in several containers of Bromophos.) But I grow my carrots in drills, leaving space not only for weeding but also for mulching (with seaweed), if mulching becomes necessary in dry weather. I bear in mind that carrots grown in crowded beds never reach any great size.

I sow the early varieties in March and the main crop in April. Sometimes, in June and early July, I put in two more drills of 'earlies', for succession, in ground from which, for example, an early crop of peas has been taken.

Jean favours carrots not only because she likes their taste but also because she believes they are the most nutritious of all our root vegetables. My mother and grandmother believed this, too, though Humphrey Davy reckoned that parsnips were equally good.

Jean has a further notion that carrots help the eyesight. During World War II it was put about that British night-fighter pilots owed their victories to a diet of carrots. Here may exist a hint of truth, but I suspect that radar was the main cause of their success in shooting down enemy planes in the dark.

Almost without exception the herbalists were – and are – enthusiastic about carrots. They claim that they increase the number of red corpuscles in the blood – a claim supported by scientists in the World Health Organisation – and that they are the best remedy for liver complaints. Some of us who like a dram ought, perhaps, to reflect upon this. Might not carrot juice after a Burns Supper be more effective than 'a hair of the dog'?

At one time carrots were given credit for being slightly aphrodisiac. Boorde, in his *Dyetary*, writes: 'Caretes soden and eaten doth auge and increase nature, and doth cause a man to make water.' To some of us on whom old age is creeping up this advice would appear to be counterproductive. But Lemery, in his *Treatise on All Sorts of Food*, published in 1745, declares also that they are 'sodorifick, good for Wounds, opening, proper for the Stone and help Womens Terms'.

I looked up 'sodorifick' in a medical dictionary and found that 'sudorific' means 'producing copious perspiration'. (When I think of what all kinds of experts – especially gardening experts – are going to say about the quality of this book, the writing of it has become for me definitely 'sodorifick'.)

French grannies used to make a mash with raw carrots, grated and moistened with lemon juice. With this they anointed their faces, leaving it on for half an hour, in the belief that it cleared the complexion, got rid of blotches and small spots and combated wrinkles.

I wonder if my granny, who had a beautiful complexion, knew about this. According to my mother, she did use carrot juice for my grandfather's indigestion.

Cauliflower

Mark Twain described the cauliflower as 'a cabbage with a college education'. Culpeper found it less 'windy' and in describing its health-giving properties made no snide references to bagpipes or bellows.

Cauliflowers grow well enough at the Mull of Kintyre, especially the early varieties which are ready for use in July and August. In my experience, however, later varieties are even more susceptible to the brassica pests than cabbages and have to be given a great deal of cosseting. Cabbages are tough, like street urchins. Cauliflowers are delicate and appreciate constant attention from a nanny or a governess.

In sandy ground they also require plentiful watering:

otherwise they tend to go limp and colourless, like puny child-ren in the sun.

A chubby cauliflower, popped into boiling water, cooked for as short a time as possible and then served with a cheese sauce makes a delicious and balanced meal. So Jean tells me. But I must admit I prefer it simply as a vegetable on its own, to accompany chicken or lamb. It is so tasty in itself that in my opinion no kind of sauce is needed at all. But for some reason all the womenfolk I know (including Jean) are inveterate sauce makers and so, as a rule, I have to remain silent when cauli-flower is served with a plain flour sauce, flavoured with grated cheese, salt and pepper.

The Romans were equally concerned with 'improving' a taste which, as far as I am concerned, 'needs no bush'. They took 'the most tender and delicate parts [of the cauliflower] which are boiled with that extreme care the artist always devotes to his finest operations; and afterwards, when the water has been drained off, add cummin, pepper, chopped onions and coriander seed – all bruised together, not forget-ting, before serving up, to add a little oil and sun-made wine'.

All well and good. But I believe the cauliflower ought to be allowed to speak for itself.

Leeks

Did you know that leeks are of the same family as lilies? I did not until told so by a gardening expert with whom I once shared a programme on Scottish Television.

Like all faithful gardeners he was eager to convey knowl-edge to anybody who showed interest, and that afternoon I learned more about leeks than I had previously learned in half a century. The wonder is that he was born and bred in a city and had worked in a city garden all his life, unexposed to country lore. In this perhaps he was fortunate.

Leeks are the hardiest of all vegetables, he told me. They stand blustering winters well and grow on in the spring. They are susceptible to no particular pests and require little water-ing, except at transplanting time.

'You make them sound ideal for Achnamara garden,' I said.

'Yes. Though in your sandy ground you will have to dig plenty of dung and seaweed into the plot before planting them out. And they're such greedy little beggars that they demand long drinks of liquid manure every week.'

'What kind of liquid manure?'

'Well, you're lucky in that your friend, Richard Semple, can supply you with dung. Rummle up a graipful of that in a bucket of water and there you have it.'

Everything he said is true. I sow the seed in my 'nursery' in early March. It takes a long time to germinate, but I have learned not to panic and make further sowings, and eventually when the green does appear, growth is strong and quick. In June or early July I transplant them, dibbling them in deep with plenty of water. On my expert's advice I trim their leaves with a pair of scissors, so as to encourage white growth and, later on, for the same purpose, earth up the growing plants. (People who prefer more green in their leeks should disregard this advice.)

Jeans says that leeks are an essential ingredient of winter broth. I believe her. In Scotland all good cooks know the secret of making 'cockaleeky'. Basically a chicken stock augmented by large quantities of chopped leeks, it is nearly always served as the soup course at Burns Suppers. Why Burns never wrote a poem about 'cockaleeky' I cannot understand. It was as much a part of his country diet as 'parritch' and haggis.

Not long ago, on television, I saw that delightful comedian Max Boyce brandishing his enormous leek and reminding us all that it is the emblem of Wales. This made me wonder: have leeks always been particularly favoured by the Celtic races? Anglo-Saxon herbalists, I fear, strew subtle hints in this direction.

Evelyn writes: 'The Welsh, who eat them much, are observed to be very fruitful.' Lemery supposes that the leek 'stops Vapours, and prevents drunkenness. It is externally applied for the stinging of Serpents and for burns and piles.' But perhaps, as a Celt, I am imagining slights where none was intended.

In fact the leek was chosen as the emblem of Wales for a historical reason. In the year AD 640 the Britons under

Cadwallader won a great victory over the Saxons 'by the judicious regulation adopted for rendering the Britons known to each other, by wearing Leeks in their caps . . . while the Saxons, for the want of such a distinguishing mark, frequently mistook each other, and dealt their fury among themselves'.

Lettuce

A lettuce is a simple, uncomplicated vegetable. The gardener finds it easy to grow. The housewife has no worries concerning its prepartion for the table. This may be why it was as popular among the ancients as it is among the moderns.

It was mentioned in Chinese manuscripts of the seventh century BC. And Theophrastus, writing in the third century BC, says that it 'purgeth away dropsy and takes away dimness of sight and nervous ulcers in the eye, for which purpose it is administered in human milk'.

Twentieth-century gardeners can do no better than follow the advice of Palladius, who lays down that lettuce should be grown 'in a manured, fat, moist and dunged ground: it must be sowen in faire weather in places where there is plenty of water'.

I sow some All the Year Round in the 'nursery' as early as possible: as early, indeed, as the last week of February if the weather is mild. (On the same day I usually plant shallots.) The aim is to have a salad, with lettuce, at the beginning of May, and, if no drought or excessive heat occurs, I fairly regularly hit the mark.

I used to thin my lettuces like turnips and carrots, throwing away the thinnings. This I find to be extravagant. I continue to thin them, leaving, say, about a dozen plants in the original row to mature *in situ*; but now, using as always plenty of water, I transfer the sturdiest of the thinnings to a corner of the main plot. These are checked by the transplant, but in about a week they are well established again and provide an ideal 'succession' to the 'nursery' crop.

Three further sowings (one of All the Year Round and two of Webb's Wonderful), following the transplant procedure, keep the salad bowl full until well into the winter.

Another thing I have learned about lettuce: too much dung

and too many 'artificials' can result in plants outgrowing themselves and splitting up into seeding 'families'. Palladius was a great advocate of manure and dung – in a general sense quite rightly in my opinion – but as far as lettuce is concerned I reckon it grows best in ground which has been well dunged for a previous crop, such as potatoes.

In olden days lettuce was supposed to have an effect the opposite of aphrodisiac. For example, when Adonis died, Venus flung herself down in a lettuce bed 'to cool her desires'. (Why has no artist limned so delectable a picture?) And Culpeper says that it represses 'venerous dreams'. The odd fact is that modern homeopaths use lettuce to treat impotence.

Mint

Mint is like alstroemeria. Its roots crawl and increase like worms, and you plant it at your peril. It needs no dung, no 'artificials', just a shady nook and an occasional watering.

There are two methods of control. Each year you rip out the shoots which threaten to engulf all your other vegetables, or, more expertly, you plant mint in a large fish-box sunk in the ground, the bottom and sides of which, in theory, will prevent the roots from spreading into forbidden territory. If you do not have my luck in being able to collect discarded fish-boxes from the shore then an old bucket will do, provided that you knock holes in it for drainage purposes.

Neither of these methods is a guarantee of success. I have tried both.

My mint flourishes under the only tree (with the exception of three ornamental conifers) which has survived at Achnamara. It is a hardy plane tree, becoming leafier each year, and the mint appreciates the shade and shelter that it gives. In dealing with rogue shoots of mint I used to scramble among its twigs and branches, a bruised and battered creature, and found it all too easy to relinquish the task of uprooting before it was properly done. Subsequently, visitors would point out, laughing, that mint was growing among my potatoes or my onions, a humbling sign they would suggest of my ineptitude as a gardener.

For a time, when I tried the fish-box method, it appeared to be working well. Then one day in summer I observed to my dismay that little shoots of mint were popping up all round its edges, the roots having cleverly, like moles, found their way through the drainage holes. Once again I had to fight my way under the plane tree and do some savage uprooting.

However, it can be argued that mint is well worth all the trouble it causes. Jean would never be without it, and neither would I, especially on a cool summer evening, when a mouth-watering odour of roasting lamb is wafted out from the kitchen.

Classical writers and herbalists seem to have liked mint, too. Its very name has a legendary significance.

The story goes that a young nymph called Minthe, whose father, would you believe, was the river Cocytus, one day encountered Pluto, who proceeded, not uncharacteristically, to make love to her. But Pluto had a regular girlfriend, Proserpine, a jealous creature, who observed the ploy and, before anything serious could happen, changed Minthe into a plant growing at the riverside.

For Pluto it must have been a frustrating experience – and a traumatic one for Minthe. Why, I wonder, did not Proserpine provide them both with a nice damp bed of lettuce, which would have served her purpose in a civilized and much less cruel way? Such human reactions, of course, were often ignored by classical writers. Their main purpose in telling this story was to explain why mint likes damp ground near streams.

Pliny recommends that students should bind their heads in crowns of plaited mint, 'for it delighteth the soul and is there-fore good for the mind'. I suggested to Jean that whilst writing this book I might well be inspired by such a crown, especially if it was plaited by a loving wife.

'You know, of course, what the Greeks said about mint?' she inquired.

'Were they interested, too?'

'Of course. They inferred that it so incites a man to love that it diminishes his courage.'

'Catch twenty-two,' I said and left it at that.

In the ninth century the German abbot, Strabo, made a

remarkable claim. 'If one wished to tell completely all the virtues, species and names of mint,' he writes, 'one would have to be able to say how many fishes swim in the Red Sea or the number of sparks Vulcan can count flying up from the vast furnaces of Etna.'

There are, indeed, many species of mint. They include wild mint, round-leaved mint, apple mint, peppermint, curled mint, balm mint, brandy mint, horse mint, water mint, corn mint, hairy mint, whorled mint, spearmint, mackerel mint and penny royal. Until recently I have been content to grow the ordinary garden mint. But when my friend from Barnard Castle, Parkin Raine, offered me some roots of apple mint I was glad to give them lodging under the plane tree. They have grown into magnificent plants, and both Jean and I enjoy their flavour.

Herbalists have always found in mint therapeutic virtues. My granny had great faith in it as a cure for digestive disorders, notably flatulence. So had my mother. She often added a few mint leaves to cabbages and peas, 'to prevent the wind'. An old recipe book which came from the manse and is now part of my 'curiosity library' describes an infusion 'to combat sluggishness of the stomach and bowels, prevent flatulence and stimulate the gall bladder'. It consists of half-a-dozen leaves of mint in a cupful of boiling water, left to infuse for five minutes and taken twice a day after meals. Many a time, as boys, we were subjected to this treatment. It was more palatable than castor oil and certainly did us no harm.

I believe that mashes of mint leaves, softened in lukewarm water, were once used as compresses for migraine, facial neuralgia and rheumatic pains. They were probably as beneficial as many of the modern drugs and would have no evil side effects.

One last word from Culpeper: 'Mint cureth the bite of a mad dog.' Will the World Health Organisation put this theory to a practical test?

Onions

For a time, during World War II, I soldiered in the Middle East, mainly in Iran, or Persia as we called it then. Whenever we were lucky enough to receive fresh rations they nearly always included onions, which we ate raw with our 'hard tack' biscuits and slabs of the usual soapy cheese. I was reminded of a historian's claim that Alexander the Great had fed onions to his troops, in order to 'increase their martial ardour'.

I am afraid they had no such effect on me or on my 'Jocks'. We were all willing enough to serve our country; but the idea of killing for it (and being killed) was never something that aroused us to wild enthusiasm. We responded ably enough, though dourly, when Churchill and Monty encouraged us to 'hit the Nazis for six'. But we would much rather have been eating onions at home, in the peaceful environs of Ayrshire or Argyll, inciting the Rangers to hit Celtic for six (or *vice versa*). Why, we wondered in our simple way, could governments (of most countries in the world) never understand that the dearest wish of ordinary folk is to live at peace with one another? Why did our so-called 'leaders' always seem to give such a high priority to manufacturing guns for us to use against one another and such a low priority to our physical and spiritual well-being and the ideal of friendship between all men?

But to return to our onions.

Unlike Alexander the Great, some Roman generals forbade their use, because they suspected that onions inclined their soldiers towards 'dalliance'. Their naïveté does not surprise me. Generals (in general, you understand) have never been noted for their keen understanding of the human situation. My Fusiliers required no stimulus, such as an onion, to incline them towards 'dalliance', if the opportunity arose. In any case, did it never occur to the Roman generals that their men, breath stinking of onions, might be hard put to it to persuade any female to 'dally' with them?

A widely held belief is that onions guard against infectious diseases. My granny told my mother that when boiled in milk they are an effective remedy for colds and sneezes. The World Health Organisation would probably endorse such advice. They have established scientifically that the juices in an onion are antiseptic. (Which, of course, has been known for centuries.)

The herbalists have always argued that the onion is the most important item in 'natural medicine'.

Jean Palaiseul writes: 'It is tonic, diuretic, vermifuge, emollient and antiseptic. . . . It has been used as a prophylactic during epidemics of plague and cholera . . . and it has been put forward as a contributory factor of longevity – the Bulgarians, it is pointed out, are great eaters of onions and count many centenarians among their number; it has been said that it lends colour to the hair and fosters hair-growth; it has been recommended for obesity. ("You who are fat and lymphatic," we read in one treatise, "eat raw onion, it was for you that God made it!").'

And of course it has been praised as an aphrodisiac. What vegetable has *not* been praised as an aphrodisiac? After a 'night on the tiles', the traditional remedy for a man about to go home to his wife or girlfriend is a large bowl of onion soup. And there is the humorous custom, once observed in Scotland, of bringing pots of onion soup to a young couple after their wedding night. (Nowadays most honeymoon couples disappear at once to Mediterranean islands, leaving jokey neighbours, if they are so inclined, to drink the onion soup themselves.)

It took me some time – and grievous trial and error – to discover a way of producing good onions.

I started by attempting to grow them from seed. This may be done by sowing in late summer and planting out in spring. But my first essay in this direction was thwarted by winter gales and an unusual frost. Most of my tender plants died and those which survived, when planted out in the following March, were soon attacked by white rot and the onion fly. In the end I found myself the possessor of no more than about half-a-dozen bulbs. And I succeeded in destroying those, too, by pulling them up and cutting off the foliage while it was still green. Jean was able to use one or two of them but the rest soon became rotten.

So then I asked advice and acquired a gardening book. I learned that as far as onions are concerned I had committed every sin known to nature.

In the context of my kind of garden the sowing of onions is a bad bet. Much better to grow them from sets which may be planted early in March in ground thoroughly dunged and limed – and treated with Bromophos to repel the onion fly. In my new state of enlightenment I also dip each set, as I plant it, in a calomel paste as an insurance against white rot.

As the plants mature – sometimes in late July but more often in August – I bend them over at the neck to stop them growing. Towards the end of August I ease them out of the ground and leave them for a few days to lie basking in the sun. (Wait for the sun. It will come eventually, as it always does at harvest time.) Then, when the bulbs are thoroughly dry, I transfer them to the loft – withering foliage left uncut – where they rest, dry and airy, on a hammock of windbreak until Jean needs them for the pot.

I grow plenty of shallots, too, taking similar precautions. They are ready for eating much earlier than onions, and both bulbs and foliage can be used to happy effect in salads.

> Let onion atoms lurk within the bowl,
> And, scarce suspected, animate the whole.

The flavour of shallots is mild, which is why some gourmets prefer them to onions. The fat and fictional American detective, Nero Wolfe, who never allowed the intricacies of a 'case' to interfere with his regular intake of superbly cooked food, sometimes had shallots flown from Europe to enhance his enjoyment of a special soup or stew.

Old Alec did not share Nero Wolfe's enthusiasm. 'Shallots!' he used to say. 'Nae taste at a'! Shallots is jeest hauf-he'rted onions that breed like bloody rabbits!'

But Jean and I like them as a cooked vegetable in June and July before the onions are ripe. And our neighbours, Denis and Heather Dryden, eat them raw with salt.

Spring onions, sown for succession, last with us for most of the year. When our nephew-in-law, Bill Gidlow, arrives from Leicestershire I always put a special pile of them on his side-plate. Otherwise he would leave none in the salad for the rest of us.

Before raw onions (of whatever kind) are eaten on a regular basis, it is recommended that your stomach should be in good order and strong enough to deal with them. After all, as my granny believed, they are good, cut in half, for cleaning windows and knife blades. They can also be used for adding a shine to patent leather belts and handbags. And, mixed with a little damp earth, a handful of crushed onions is said to be excellent for cleaning brasses.

Parsley

Parsley has the reputation of being the most difficult of all herbs to grow. An English proverb suggests that the best time to sow it is on Good Friday when you come home from church. If you utter several deep-throated curses at the same time you can be fairly certain it will germinate. Even so, however, it first goes down seven times to the Devil and back again.

I have never had any difficulty in growing parsley. Being a minister's son and having served throughout World War II with a Lowland Scots regiment, I now possess a wide vocabulary of swearwords, and this may be one reason for my success. I do find, however, that parsley takes an unconscionable time to come up.

I sow it in small clumps in various odd corners. The soil has to be reasonably well dunged and dug, but no antipest precautions are necessary, in my case at least. When old Alec cleaned his chimney he used to spread soot on his parsley ground – and, indeed, on his carrot ground as well. He always had good parsley; but his carrots seldom survived the usual 'fly' attack.

Parsley roots produce tender foliage for two years. After that it runs to seed and the taste becomes more bitter, or 'wersher', as we say in Scotland. I make new sowings every second spring; but some gardeners (especially in England) prefer to do this yearly, in April, July and February, to ensure continuing young and tender twigs.

A considerable mythology has accumulated around parsley. In his *Dyetary* Boorde writes: 'The Rootes of percelly soden tender, and made in a Succade, is good for the Stone, and doth make men to pysse.' (Carrots also, according to Mr Boorde, 'cause a man to make water'. Does this curious interest in micturition indicate that he himself had a faulty bladder?)

Parsley featured importantly at ancient Greek funerals, when it was sprinkled on the corpse. There was – and still may be – a Greek saying about a person on the point of death: 'He is in need of parsley.'

Roman writers praised it. 'Parsley is in great request,' wrote Pliny, 'and no man there is but loveth it: for nothing is the more ordinary than to see large branches of Parsley good store swimming in their potage.'

Henry VIII was fond of roast 'conny' (rabbit). He ate it with a special sauce made of 'percelly minced small' and boiled with butter and 'verjuice' (cider vinegar) and seasoned with sugar and a little pepper.

Experts in nutrition, including those in the World Health Organisation, have found parsley to be rich in iron, calcium, vitamins and various trace elements essential to good health. A French specialist writes: 'One may, without exaggeration, consider it as one of the most valuable health-giving food-stuffs that nature has generously put at the disposal of mankind. Do not hesitate to use it freely, cooked or raw.'

My granny said much the same thing to my mother. In the Gaelic.

Parsnips

The Russian word for a parsnip is 'pasternak'. Would *Doctor Zhivago* have had such a triumph in the English-speaking world had the author been publicized as Mr Parsnip? Jasper Carrot has won richly deserved success. But then, he is a comedian.

Until the middle of last century parsnips in Britain grew 'wild' and were not cultivated in gardens. Writing in 1629, however, Parkinson says of them: 'The root is a great nourisher, and is much more used in the time of Lent, being boyled and stewed with butter, than in any other time of the year.' Tournefort (in 1719) explains that parsnips are sweetest in Lent 'by reason the juice has been concocted during the winter, and they are desired at that season especially, both for their agreeable taste and their wholesomeness; they are not so good in any respect, till they have been first nipt with cold.' Old Alec and my mother would have agreed with Tournefort. Both believed that parsnips should not be eaten until they have been properly matured during the winter. They had another curious idea – which, for all I know, may be perfectly valid – that the roots contain strychnine. By spring the amount of poison has been reduced to a safe and, indeed, tonic dose.

The parsnip so widely cultivated today was evolved from the wild ones by selection. The best and most palatable was produced by a Professor Buchman about 1850. He called it the 'Student' and from it have come most of the modern varieties.

Jock has a passion for parsnips. Though Jean and I like them occasionally in stews, those in my garden are mainly reserved for him during his holidays from reporting golf.

They grow well at Achnamara and appear to be impervious to attack by gremlins of any kind. 'Sow early in February, wi' plenty o' coo shit,' was Old Alec's advice. I have found no reason to question it.

Peas

An old-fashioned English rhyme makes a prediction:

> On Candlemass Day if the thorns hang adrop,
> Then you are sure of a good pea crop.

On 2 February, at the Mull of Kintyre, the hawthorns are seldom without the tears caused by our climate. Perhaps this is one reason why my pea crop seldom fails. Another reason may be that peas do not require rich soil. Sandy ground into which has been dug plenty of dung and potash-rich seaweed for root vegetables in the previous year seems to be ideal for them, though, preferring to be on the safe side rather than sorry, I usually scatter handfuls of a general fertilizer along the drills.

The pea moth is a gremlin which sometimes chews little holes in the leaves, but an insecticide spray when the flowers are forming keeps it from becoming a serious menace.

In 1984, from the third week in April until about the middle of July, Southend experienced an unusual amount of hot, dry weather. An April temperature of 70°F was something unprecedented in our area. For many weeks it remained around the same mark, allowing us all to acquire Bermudan tans.

Flowers and vegetables enjoyed the sun, too, provided they were given an evening drink. Our lawn, without sprinklers, was the only real sufferer, drying up into a patchwork of brown and pale green. This did not unduly worry me. I had less mowing to do. But towards the end of May the three rows of peas (Meteors), sown at three-weekly intervals for succession, were beginning to show signs of distress, the foliage dry and blotched with white. Flowers were sparse and seemed reluctant to bloom.

My brother Willie was holidaying with us at the time. 'No problem,' he told me. 'Put a couple of tablespoonfuls of sulphate of ammonia in a two-gallon can of water and irrigate the roots. A can to each drill. Repeat in three or four days.' (Though now retired, he has not lost his sea-captain's way of issuing orders.)

I took his advice. After all, he declares he is the best and, arguably, the only real gardener in the family. Now I am prepared to admit that his boast may be no idle one. My peas perked up at once. And in July and August Jean and I picked and podded the finest crop we have ever had.

We have no freezer of our own. But our neighbour, Heather Dryden – daughter of my horticultural guru, Robertson Finlayson – sometimes lets Jean have the use of hers. (As in every good community, in Southend we exchange goods and services as the need arises, without interference from tax men or chartered accountants.) As a result of this arrangement we were assured, in 1984, of having young and tender peas with our Christmas dinner.

In former times peas were dried rather than frozen. My granny did this, and her family was fed as much on pease brose as on porridge. My mother once tried it out on us, when we were children, encouraged by the Padre, whose own mother, in North Uist, had made pease brose, too.

'Great stuff for the bowels,' he told us.

The experiment, however, was not a success. We hated the taste. Archie and Willie, infants of five and three respectively, spat it out. Being in a position of responsibility as the eldest brother (aged nine at the time) I did my best to swallow it. But the Padre, as usual, had the last word.

'Take it away, Mama. You don't know how to cook it!'

I am still uncertain, therefore, about the value of pease brose as a bowel-mover.

Its English equivalent was pease pudding. The rural poet, Thomas Tusser, who died in 1580 after a lifetime spent in the study of farming and gardening (*vide* his book, *Five Hundred Points of Good Husbandry*), had something to say on the subject:

> Good peason and leeks, to make porredge in Lent,
> And peascods in July, save fish to be spent.
> Those having, with other things, plentifull then
> Thou winnest the love of the labouring men.

He also offered some advice: 'Make hunger thy sauce, as a medicine for health.'

Green peas floating in a steaming plate of Scotch broth make me hungry just to look at them.

Radishes

The Egyptian pyramid workers were fed on garlic, onions and radishes. 'Huge quantities' of radishes, according to the scribes. Poor devils. How, on such a diet, they were able to hoist such enormous stones into position remains as much a mystery to me as the real purpose of the pyramids themselves.

And when I consider the thousands upon thousands of builders employed in their construction, it is difficult for me to imagine the vast acreages which must have been necessary for the cultivation, in succession, of 'huge quantities' of radishes. Not to mention all that garlic and all those onions.

Ancient Egyptian gardeners must have had a highly profitable time. And yet, as far as I know, they do not figure prominently among the hieroglyphics. Some of them must have retired as millionaires, like the legendary McConnachie, who supplied rations to the troops in World War I.

The Greeks, according to historians, kept a golden radish in the temple at Delphi. The reason for this I have yet to discover. And Pliny tells us that the Romans extracted oil from radish seed, though his opinion of the root itself was not high. 'A vulgar article of the diet,' he remarks in his dogmatic way.

The old herbalists, as might be expected, had plenty to say about radishes. Evelyn, for example, believed that they repel 'the Vapours of Wine, when the Wits are at their genial Club'. Another theory was that they 'drive the Stone out of the kidneys and the Bladder, and are good for the Cholic in the Back'. And yet another: 'If radishes be cut close to the wane of the moon, they will cure Corns on the Feet.' (Strangely enough, Mr Boorde does not claim that they cause him 'to pysse'.)

As always, however, herbalists have a vision of the truth. For some time now, as a specific for liver complaints, a black radish extract has been sold by chemists under the name of *raphanus*. And recently the World Health Organisation has confirmed that radishes are a true specific for disorders of the gall bladder and the liver. Next time you find black radish rings in a *hors d'oeuvre* do not despise them.

I like radishes in the salad bowl. Jean has no great taste for them. Since they are easily grown, however, and mature quickly (in about four to six weeks after sowing) I cultivate a few for the benefit of occasional visitors, like Jock, who are fond of them.

They do well in sandy soil which has been well dunged and watered. This is probably one reason why they were so popular with the Egyptians, who had the desert on one side and the Nile on the other – and a multitude of camels.

Turnips

In America swedes are called rotabuga, from the Swedish *rotabugge* ('red bags'). But most people, including Jean and myself – and Jock when he is at home – love turnips, mashed or in a stew.

I find them difficult to grow, because, as I have already pointed out, I have not yet discovered a defence against certain little white bugs which burrow into them during the summer. They do not attack the bottom or sides of the turnip. They chew their way in at the leaf joints.

The odd and embarrassing thing is that my neighbours are faced with no such problem. Their Purple Top Milans, their Snowballs and their Golden Balls grow clean and tender, while later sowings in my garden, if left in the ground for any length of time, often deteriorate into brown sap.

While being able to claim a modest triumph in the general battle against gremlins, I am worried and harassed by this continuing guerilla activity. Some day an expert may find pity in his heart and indicate to a fumbling amateur the right kind of weapon (or weapons) to use in a counterattack.

I have never had unqualified success with my turnips. In the beginning they grew scrawny and wooden, in spite of the fact that in those days the white bugs were not in evidence. Then Robertson Finlayson pointed out that my ground was acid and that turnips more than most vegetables – except perhaps the brassicas – require not only plenty of manure but also plenty of lime. Since that time my turnips have grown well enough; but the white bugs have seldom failed to create damage among those not harvested by June at the latest.

'There's no getting blood out of a turnip,' said the poet, Frederick Marryat (1792–1848). There's no getting bugs out of mine.

The books advise deep digging for a turnip crop, with plenty of dung. I have always followed such advice; but now I am beginning to wonder if the bugs may come with – or be encouraged by – the dung.

The ancients thought highly of turnips. Theophrastus said that they run quickly to seed if a 'hot wind blows', and I have discovered this for myself, especially if they are sown too early. Now I wait until April before sowing, and they never run to seed. Unfortunately, however, the later sowings run into trouble from the bugs. A winning situation, in my garden at any rate, is difficult to establish.

Theophrastus describes how 'a desperate cough', occasioned by a continual eating of lemons, was at last cured by using a 'Decoction of Turnips'. This is the only kind of 'natural medicine' connected with turnips that I can find. Not surprising, perhaps, in view of the fact that they consist of ninety per cent water.

Though such water is delicious.

14. Rotation

It has been impressed upon me by Robertson Finlayson, my brother Willie and other experts that the rotation of crops is all-important in good vegetable gardening.

The main reason, I am told, is that different groups of crops have different soil-borne pests and diseases and by not growing one of these groups in the same place in successive years a build-up of these can – it is hoped – be prevented.

I have, therefore, divided my patch into four areas and, after much burning of midnight oil (as far as mathematical problems are concerned my IQ is low), have evolved a four-year rotation which, in theory, ought to work. (See the table overleaf.)

Does my rotation plan work?

Not always. The turnip bugs are still there. But then I sometimes become confused and sow seeds and dibble in plants in the wrong places.

I comfort myself with the dangerous thought that nature smiles more often upon human instinct than upon mathematics.

YEAR 1

Brassicas (Cabbages, sprouts, etc.) Potatoes
Legumes (Peas, beans, etc.)
Roots (Carrots, turnips, onions, leeks, etc.)
Salads (Lettuce, marrows, etc.)

YEAR 2

Legumes
Salads
Brassicas Potatoes
Roots

YEAR 3

Salads
Roots
Legumes
Brassicas Potatoes

YEAR 4

Roots
Brassicas Potatoes
Salads
Legumes

15.   But Then Face to Face

The blessed thing about a garden, from the point of view of an amateur gardener, is that he has no need of a chartered accountant to measure his success or failure. Profit and loss, in a monetary sense, is not important to him. His profit is the sweet scent of a honeysuckle flower or the sweet taste of a young turnip, both of which he has nurtured himself. His loss is the damage done to them by the gremlins which continually invade his paradise.

He is aware, of course, that behind it all there lurks a beneficent deity, calling the tune: a deity who can provide him with pleasure in work well done but who, at times, can send leaf mould or little white bugs – or even a serpent – to test his character.

As an amateur learns how to cultivate a garden properly, always helped and encouraged by interested neighbours, he finds a pleasure in life denied to cutthroat operators on stock exchanges (and in certain governments) who can never imagine success or happiness in anything not thirled to money.

It is as difficult to define the pleasure experienced by an amateur gardener as it is to define the pleasure experienced by a writer (or a golfer). If I were a poet I might be able to do it. All I can say is that it is achieved only after much hard work, many setbacks and the acceptance, in a humble way, of the fact that nature will always have the last word.

Milton had something to say on the subject.

> Beauty is nature's coin, must not be hoarded,
> But must be current, and the good thereof
> Consists in mutual and particular bliss.

The key word here is 'mutual'. Pleasure is always enhanced if gardening is carried out in a community, whether it be a community of allotment holders, of a gardening club or of a small parish like Southend. A gardener needs understanding neighbours to whom he can boast of his triumphs. He also needs them to point out his mistakes, to indicate how they may be corrected and, in certain circumstances, to jolt his pride by laughing at him.

There is happiness, too, in being able to offer fresh cut flowers or vegetables with the earth still warming their roots to friends who will appreciate them. And equal happiness in finding on the doorstep half-a-dozen sonsy swedes, left there by a neighbour who knows that your Purple Top Milans have been decimated by the bugs.

But I think the basic pleasure consists of the fact that an amateur gardener, though he may not realize it when his knees and back are aching, is reaching close to his natural condition: a condition with which poison gas and atom bombs and dictators with computers are completely out of tune.

A millionaire on his yacht in the Mediterranean contemplates with satisfaction his scotch on the rocks, his radio telephone, the diamonds glinting on his wife's fingers. But is his pleasure equal to that of a gardener, on a summer's morning, who contemplates the dewdrops glinting on the petals of his first rose: a red rose which he will soon cut and present to his wife?

The thorn of a rose is an emblem of unavoidable pain. The bush, which has to be sternly pruned to grow strong, is an emblem of his need to suffer discipline. The bloom itself is the emblem of love.

And the giving and receiving of love, as the Padre always used to tell us from his pulpit, is the greatest pleasure.

Index

Alexander the Great, 131
Alnwick, 23
Alstroemeria, 86 *et seq.*
Anchor Line, 25
Antrim, 28
Atholl Brose, 119
Atlantis, 23, 24
Ayrshire, 99

Bacon, Sir Francis, 11, 12
Barron, George, 103 *et seq.*
BBC, 103
Beechgrove Garden, 103 *et seq.*,
   123
Beetroots, 119 *et seq.*
Blackbirds, 52 *et seq.*
Boorde's *Dyetary*, 115, 123, 124,
   134
Boreham, Rev. F.W., 19
Boyce, Max, 126
Brazil, 25
Bromophos, 25, 50, 94, 121, 123,
   133
Bruce, Robert the, 61, 62
Brussels Sprouts, 120 *et seq.*
Budding, Edwin, 107
Buchman, Professor, 136
Burma, 25
Burns, Robert, 53

Cabbages, 121 *et seq.*
Caesar, Julius, 120
Cambridge, 101
Cameron, Archie, 47
Cameron, Margaret, 84
Campbeltown, 70, 79

Carrot fly, 47 *et seq.*
Carrot, Jaspar, 135
Carrots, 122, 134 *et seq.*
Caterpillars, 48
Cats, 54 *et seq.*
Cauliflowers, 124 *et seq.*
Chaucer, Geoffrey, 50
Chile, 86
City of Glasgow Bank, 101
Club-root fly, 49
Columba, Saint, 28, 33, 34, 41, 42,
   59, 68, 102
Culpepper, Nicholas, 11, 119, 121,
   124, 128, 130

Daily Express, 34, 67
Dali, Salvador, 62
Dempsey, Jack, 19
Disney, Walt, 29
Doctor Zhivago, 135
Drake, Sir Francis, 42
Druid stones, 42
Dryden, Denis, 133
Dryden, Heather, 84, 133, 137
Dumbarton, 102
Dunaverty Golf Course, 16, 103,
   108
Dunaverty Rock, 29, 41, 87, 88
Dung, use of, 45 *et seq.*
Dunoon, 24

EEC, 43
Essex, 43
Evelyn, John, 115, 126, 137

Finlayson, Robertson, 68 *et seq.*,

121, 137, 140, 141
Fleming, James Nicol, 101 *et seq*.

Gaelic Mod, 24
Galbraith, Donald, 16, 85
Gamma BHC, 25, 50, 86, 146
Gardener's Delight, 115
Gardiner, Dick, 104
Garotta, 97
Gerard, John, 115 *et seq*.
Gidlow, Bill, 133
Gigha, 27
Glasgow Evening Citizen, 67
Golden Wonders, 43
Grandmother's Secrets, 122
Gulf Stream, 23

Hawkins, Sir John, 42
Hunter, Charles, 98 *et seq*.
Hunter, Mrs Charles, 98 *et seq*.

Inverewe, 23
Iona, 35
Iran, 130
Ireland, 105

Jeyes Fluid, 98

Keil Technical School, 102
Kenmore, 25
Kew Gardens, 23
Kintyre, Mull of, 12 *et seq*., 80, 81,
    93, 109, 116, 124, 136
Kipling, Rudyard, 11 *et seq*.

Lamont, Allan, 35
Leeks, 125 *et seq*.
Leicester University, 24
Lemery, 124
Lettuces, 127 *et seq*.
Lovat Scouts, 15

McCartney, Paul, 61, 62
McColl, Jim, 103 *et seq*.
McEachran, Hugh, 80
McGill, Patrick, 63

MacKenzie, Archibald, 114 *et seq*.
MacKenzie, Mrs Archibald (Mary
    Cameron), 114 *et seq*.
McKerral, Donnie, 45
McKerral, James, 32
McKerral, Peter, 32
MacLaren, Jessie ('Maimie'), 14 *et
    seq*.
MacLeod, Rev. Kenneth, 27
MacMillan, George, 103
MacMillan, James, 84
MacMillan, Willie, 103, 108
McPhee, Jim, 47
MacVicar, Angus (junior), 25
MacVicar, Rev. Angus John ('the
    Padre'), 14 *et seq*.
MacVicar, Mrs Angus John
    ('Granny'), 14 *et seq*.
MacVicar, Angus (Jean), 27 *et seq*.
MacVicar, Archie, 15 *et seq*., 137
MacVicar, Mrs Archie (Mima), 24
MacVicar, Cameron, 25
MacVicar, Jean, 25
MacVicar, Jock, 28 *et seq*.
MacVicar, Professor John, 15 *et
    seq*.
MacVicar, Mrs John (Esmé), 25
MacVicar, Kenneth, 25
MacVicar, Rev. Kenneth, 15 *et
    seq*.
MacVicar, Mrs Kenneth (Isabel),
    25
MacVicar, Rona, 15 *et seq*.
MacVicar, Captain Willie, 15 *et
    seq*.
MacVicar, Mrs Willie (Nina), 37
Marlowe, Christopher, 109
Marryat, Frederick, 140
Milton, John, 143
Mint, 128 *et seq*.
Moles, 51 *et seq*., 61 *et seq*.
Motherwell F.C., 109

National Health Service, 39
Neolithic chambered cairns, 83
Newlands, Duncan, 79

North Carolina, 98 *et seq.*
North Uist, 15, 44, 67, 105, 137

Old Alec, 35 *et seq.*, 72, 78, 93, 133, 136
Onions, 130 *et seq.*
Onion fly, 48
Orwell George, 90

Palaiseul, Jean, 122, 132
Parsley, 134 *et seq.*
Parsnips, 135 *et seq.*
Parkinson's *Paradisi in Sole*, 115
Patrick, Saint, 103
Peas, 136 *et seq.*
Plato, 23, 24
Pliny, 11, 138
Potatoes, 41 *et seq.*

Queen Elizabeth, 115

Rabbits, 57 *et seq.*
Radishes, 138 *et seq.*
Raine, Parkin, 130
Riley, James Whitcombe, 93
Robins, 52 *et seq.*
Rotation of crops, 141 *et seq.*
Rowan trees, 37

Sackville West, V., 74
Sanda, 61, 79
Sayers, 'Bill', 87

Scarecrows, 57
Seaweed, use of, 46
Semple, Elizabeth, 35, 69
Semple, Richard, 45, 69, 126
Seymour, John, 11, 115
Shakespeare, William, 11, 20, 28, 42 *et seq.*, 77, 97, 115, 116
Shallots, 133
Sicily, 24
Soil analysis, 70 *et seq.*
Southend, parish of, 13 *et seq.*, 144
STV, 125

Taylor, Col. Hamish, 84
Theophrastus, 11, 114, 127
Tir nan Og, 23, 28
Turnips, 139 *et seq.*
Tusser, Thomas, 138
Twain, Mark, 124

Wales, 126
Walsingham, Sir Francis, 115
Watson, Duncan, 106, 111
Weather signs, 40 *et seq.*
Widdershins, planting, 28
Wilde, Oscar, 11
Wilja potatoes, 44
Wolsey, Cardinal, 90
Wordsworth, William, 107
World Health Organisation, 115 *et seq.*, 123, 130, 131, 135, 139

Bestselling Humour

☐	The Ascent of Rum Doodle	W E Bowman	£2.99
☐	Tim Brooke-Taylor's Golf Bag	Tim Brooke-Taylor	£3.99
☐	Shop! or A Store Is Born	Jasper Carrott	£2.99
☐	Cat Chat	Peter Fincham	£3.50
☐	Art of Coarse Drinking	Michael Green	£2.50
☐	Rambling On	Mike Harding	£2.50
☐	Sex Tips For Girls	Cynthia Heimel	£2.95
☐	Tales From Witney Scrotum	Peter Tinniswood	£2.50
☐	Tales From A Long Room	Peter Tinniswood	£2.75
☐	Uncle Mort's North Country	Peter Tinniswood	£2.50
☐	Five Hundred Mile Walkies	Mark Wallington	£2.50

Prices and other details are liable to change

ARROW BOOKS, BOOKSERVICE BY POST, PO BOX 29, DOUGLAS, ISLE OF MAN, BRITISH ISLES

NAME...

ADDRESS..

....

....

Please enclose a cheque or postal order made out to Arrow Books Ltd. for the amount due and allow the following for postage and packing.

U.K. CUSTOMERS: Please allow 22p per book to a maximum of £3.00.

B.F.P.O. & EIRE: Please allow 22p per book to a maximum of £3.00.

OVERSEAS CUSTOMERS: Please allow 22p per book.

Whilst every effort is made to keep prices low it is sometimes necessary to increase cover prices at short notice. Arrow Books reserve the right to show new retail prices on covers which may differ from those previously advertised in the text or elsewhere.